HIGHER
GROUND

To Dear Wee Leon.

May the Lord bless you
with humility &
continue to make
you a blessing
to many others

In His service
Kim & Johng.
Dec. 2003.

Other Neil Anderson titles published by Monarch Books:

*H*IGHER GROUND

Taking Faith To The Edge!

Dr NEIL T. ANDERSON
ROBERT SAUCY AND
DAVE PARK

MONARCH
B O O K S

First published in the USA 1998 by Harvest House Publishers,
Eugene, Oregon 97402, USA.

First published in the UK 1999 by Monarch Books.

ISBN 1 85424 465 5

British Library Cataloguing Data
A catalogue record for this book is available
from the British Library.

Designed and produced for the publisher by
Gazelle Creative Productions,
Concorde House, Grenville Place, Mill Hill, London NW7 3SA.

This book is dedicated to all those who have attended a 'Stomping Out the Darkness' student conference, love the freedom we have in Christ, and desire to walk in step with the Spirit. Keep climbing. Keep travelling onwards and upwards to higher ground!

CONTENTS

Introduction: The Treasure

God is committed to the task of conforming you and me to the image of His Son. Not physically — He's not making us look like Jesus looked physically — but inwardly in character, in patience, in gentleness, in goodness, in grace, in truth, in discipline.[1]

— *Charles Swindoll*

In Matthew 16, Jesus says:

> If anyone wishes to come after Me, let him deny himself, and take up his cross, and follow Me. For whoever wishes to save his life shall lose it; but whoever loses his life for My sake shall find it. For what will a man be profited if he gains the whole world, and forfeits his soul? Or what will a man give in exchange for his soul? For the Son of Man is going to come in the glory of His Father with His angels; and will then recompense every man according to his deeds (Matthew 16:24–27 NASB).

Following Jesus

This book is about following Jesus: learning more about denying self, taking up the cross, and giving up and taking up whatever it takes to be more like Jesus. This book is a continuation of a study in sanctification, or growing in God's grace, that first started in a book we wrote called *Radical Image*. We suggest you read *Radical Image*, but it's not a prerequisite to using *Higher Ground*. The important action for you is to begin the search for the true treasure — learning what it means to have an abundant life in Christ. This search doesn't require years of toil, like the search for silver or gold. Jesus is easy to find and totally satisfying.

Check It Out!

Give up the pleasure of things to gain the pleasure of life; give up the temporary to gain the eternal.

We like to think we can be in charge of our own lives and pursue whatever we want in life. This is just not true; we are not our own masters. The Bible tells us that we are either a slave to God or a slave to sin and Satan. Jesus said that 'everyone who commits sin is the slave of sin' (John 8:34 NASB). Romans 6:11–13 (NASB) commands us to

> consider yourselves to be dead to sin, but alive to God in Christ Jesus. Therefore do not let sin reign in your mortal body that you should obey its lusts, and do not go on presenting the members of your body to sin as instruments of unrighteousness; but present yourselves to God as those alive from the dead, and your members as instruments of righteousness to God.

Living according to the values of the ungodly world around us is the same as being a slave to Satan, for he is the god of this world (see 2 Corinthians 4:4). But we don't have to be slaves to sin; we can be free in Christ! We can choose to live a new life serving Him and doing His will. Every day we must remind ourselves that we are completely forgiven of all our sins through Christ's death on the cross. Colossians 2:13,14 from *The Message* puts it this way: 'When you were stuck in your old sin-dead life, you were incapable of responding to God. God brought you alive — right along with Christ! Think of it! All sins forgiven, the slate wiped clean, that old arrest warrant cancelled and nailed to Christ's cross.'

We've Been Set Free

Through Christ's death on the cross we have been set free from slavery to sin to live a new life for God (John 8:36). With the Spirit's help we need to make the daily choice to put to death the deeds of our flesh and follow Jesus (Romans 8:13). The decision to follow Jesus is ours alone. No one can make that choice for us — no youth pastor and not even mum or dad! The power to follow Jesus comes only from the Holy Spirit who lives inside us. If we are not led by the Spirit, we will soon get tired of resisting temptation, and we'll give in to sin (Romans 8:9–14). Colossians 3:10,11 says we 'have put on the new self, which is being renewed in knowledge in the image of its Creator. Here there is no Greek or Jew, circumcised or uncircumcised, barbarian, Scythian, slave or free, but Christ is all, and is in all.' In other words, how we used to identify ourselves no longer applies. We don't look back to the fact that we were sinful or came from a non-Christian family; we look to who we are in Christ. We don't look to anything to get our identity, even if it appears good. You're not good or holy because you do good things. You're holy only through Christ's death, burial, and resurrection. Our identity lies in the fact that we are now children of God and that we are in Christ. A Christian, in terms of his or her deepest identity, is a saint: a new creation, a divine masterpiece, a child of light, a citizen of heaven. Take a second to soak in who you really are in Christ and read out loud these thoughts:

'I am a child of God' (John 1:12).

'I am Jesus' chosen friend' (John 15:15).

'I am holy and acceptable [justified] to God' (Romans 5:1).

'I am united to the Lord, and I am one spirit with Him' (1 Corinthians 3:16).

'I have been bought with a price. I belong to God' (1 Corinthians 6:19,20).

'I am a part of the body of Christ, part of His family' (1 Corinthians 12:27).

'I am a saint, a holy one' (Ephesians 1:1).

'I have been adopted as God's child' (Ephesians 1:5).

'I have been bought back (redeemed) and forgiven of all my sins' (Colossians 1:14).

'I am complete in Christ' (Colossians 2:10).

'I am free forever from the law of sin and death' (Romans 8:1,2).

'I know all things work together for good' (Romans 8:28).

'I am free from any condemning charges against me' (Romans 8:33–39).

'I cannot be separated from the love of God' (Romans 8:35–39).

'I am hidden with Christ in God' (Colossians 3:3).

'I am sure that the good work God has started in me will be finished' (Philippians 1:6).

'I am a citizen of heaven with the rest of God's family' (Ephesians 2:19).

'I can find grace and mercy in times of need' (Hebrews 4:16).

'I am born of God, and the evil one cannot touch me' (1 John 5:18).

We are no longer a product of our past. We are now the handiwork of Jesus. And what He did on the cross for us gives us a new identity and a new way to live. We are now free to grow in God's grace and be all that God has called us to be. Growing up isn't easy, but God has given us everything we need to live abundant lives through Christ.

Climbing to Higher Ground

What happened when you became a child of God through faith in Jesus? Did anything really change inside you? Satan, and maybe a few of your so-called friends, wants you to believe you are the same messed-up piece of sinful humanity you were before you trusted Christ. But that is not true. No Way! God sees you as you really are — His child alive in Christ. That is your position: joined to Jesus Christ and united with His life. Even though you may not feel like a new creation in Christ, you are actually a whole new person inside.

—————————— Check It Out! ——————————

When temptation strikes, will you be able to stand firm in the knowledge that you're God's holy child? Will you do what Jesus would do? Climb to higher ground and grow deeper in your relationship with Christ.

Do you see yourself as a weak and struggling Christian who just can't seem to get it together? God sees you as His dear child, holy and blameless, with everything you need to walk in victory! Who's right? God is! You see, deep down inside the real you is 'in Christ'! You are forgiven, free from sin's grip and united to the One who has all authority and power. Now you are able to hear His voice, understand His Word, follow Him and grow in Christ.

It's one thing to listen to a message or read a book and nod your head and say, 'Okay! I believe that I am dead to sin. I can say no to sin and yes to God.' It's a completely different ball game actually to live it! What will you do when temptation strikes? What do you do now? When temptations and trials come, that's when we have to choose to believe the truth about who we are in Christ and live like Jesus — actually to do what Jesus would do. It's one thing to think, 'What would Jesus do?' Anyone can wear a 'WWJD' T-shirt or bracelet and think or ask that question, but actually to live a life that is a true reflection of God's holy character — that's what Jesus is really after in our lives.

We are rewarded every day as we follow Jesus and experience His presence. What would you give in exchange for love, joy, and peace? Would you sell out Jesus to be rich? Give up His leading or hearing His voice for silver? Would you trade the treasures that last forever for a single hot meal? I don't think so! Don't sell out your birthright! Don't be like Esau, who traded his birthright for a hot lunch. (See Genesis 25:29–34.) Instead, understand how much God loves you, and enjoy the abundant life He has prepared for you. It's our hope that this book will help you discover more about who you are in Christ, learn to walk in His ways, and to become more like Him. We invite you to hit the trail and start climbing to *higher ground*.

God's love for you is not dependent on how [you] look, how [you] think, how you act, or how perfect you are. His love is absolutely non-negotiable and non-returnable. Ours is a faithful God. No matter what you do, no matter how far you fall, no matter how ugly you become, God is relentless, undying, unfathomable, unquenchable love from which you cannot be separated. Ever! Run to Jesus. Jesus wants you to go to Him. He wants to become the most important thing in your life, the greatest love you'll ever know. He wants you to love him so much that there's no room in your heart and in your life for sin.[1]

— *Max Lucado*

1

Life-Changing Stuff — Making Truth Personal

Have you ever started to read a book or watch a TV show where they began to use a lot of words and terms that no one without a double Ph.D. in nuclear physics could possibly understand? It's frustrating, isn't it? It's like those medical shows on TV, *'Doctor, we have to cauterise the bifurcation of the subterminal of the left ventricle before a massive haematoma leads to major fibrillation and eventually coma.'* I have no idea what I just wrote but it sounds bad. It would be nice if somebody gave us a list of what some of those medical terms meant. Well someone took a shot at it and here is what they came up with![2]

- *Artery:* The study of painting
- *Bacteria:* The backdoor of the cafeteria
- *Barium:* What doctors do when their patients die
- *Bowel:* A letter like A, E, I, O, or U
- *Caesarean Section:* A neighbourhood in Rome
- *CAT Scan:* Searching for a kitty
- *Coma:* punctuation mark
- *Cauterise:* To make eye contact with a girl
- *Enema:* Someone who is not your friend
- *Fester:* Quicker
- *Fibula:* A small lie
- *Labour pain:* When you get hurt at work
- *Nitrates:* Cheaper than day rates
- *Node:* Was aware of
- *Outpatient:* A patient who fainted
- *Pelvis:* An Elvis impersonator
- *Recovery room:* A place to do upholstery
- *Rectum:* Almost killed 'em
- *Secretion:* Something you don't want anyone to know
- *Seizure:* A Roman emperor
- *Tablet:* A small table
- *Terminal:* Where planes land
- *Urine:* Opposite of 'You're out'
- *Varicose:* Nearby
- *Vein:* To be conceited

I think they might have misinterpreted a few words! In this book you might come across some terms that might throw you for a few seconds, but hang in there. Many people are easily confused about the concepts of salvation and sanctification because both are presented in the Bible in the past, present, and future verb tenses. Remember that English class you took? Well here is where you put some of that stuff to work. The Bible says we *have been* saved, we *are presently* being saved, and we *will* someday be fully saved. Notice the past tenses (italics) in the following verses declaring that in Christ we have been saved:

Because of his great love for us, God, who is rich in mercy, *made* us alive with Christ even when we were dead in transgressions — it is by grace you *have been saved....* It is by grace you *have been* saved, through faith — and this not from yourselves, it is the gift of God (Ephesians 2:4,5,8).

Join with me in suffering for the gospel, by the power of God, who *has saved* us and called us to a holy life — not because of anything we have done but because of his own purpose and grace (2 Timothy 1:8,9).

When the kindness and love of God our Saviour appeared, he *saved* us, not because of righteous things we had done, but because of his mercy. He *saved* us through the washing of rebirth and renewal by the Holy Spirit (Titus 3:4,5).

These verses clearly teach that *every* child of God has experienced salvation. We have been born again; consequently, we are now spiritually alive. Jesus said, 'I am the resurrection and the life. He who believes in me will live, even though he dies; and whoever lives and believes in me will never die' (John 11:25,26). In other words, because of our belief we are now spiritually alive and will stay alive even when we die physically. According to this passage, we *will never* die spiritually. Yet the Bible also tells us we are *presently* 'being saved,' as the following passages indicate:

The message of the cross is foolishness to those who are perishing, but to us who *are being* saved it is the power of God (1 Corinthians 1:18).

We are to God the aroma of Christ among those who *are being* saved and those who *are perishing* (2 Corinthians 2:15).

My dear friends, as you have always obeyed — not only in my presence, but now much more in my absence —

continue to work out your salvation with fear and trembling (Philippians 2:12).

We do not work *for* our salvation, but we are called to work *out* what God has brought to birth in us. As we will see later, there is a progressive aspect of sanctification that is similar in concept to the continuing process of salvation. That is, we are 'being saved,' and we are presently being conformed to the image of God. Our salvation begins on earth, but it is completed in heaven. That is why the Bible speaks about a future aspect of salvation. Look at the following passages that teach we shall be saved:

> Since we have now been justified by his blood, how much more *shall we be saved* from God's wrath (Romans 5:9).

> The hour *has come* for you to wake up from your slumber, because our salvation is nearer now than when we first believed (Romans 13:11).

> Christ was sacrificed once to take away the sins of many people; and he will appear a second time, not to bear sin, but to bring salvation to those who are waiting for him (Hebrews 9:28).

> [We have not yet been saved from the wrath that is to come, but we have the assurance that we *will be*.] Having believed, you were marked in him with a seal, the promised Holy Spirit, who is a deposit guaranteeing our inheritance until the redemption of those who are God's possession — to the praise of his glory (Ephesians 1:13,14).

Just like salvation, the biblical concept of sanctification carries us all the way from our new birth in Christ to the final perfection of glorification. The Bible clearly speaks of the believer's sanctification as *already* accomplished, as *being* accomplished, and as finally *being* completed in the future. These are often referred to as the three tenses of sanctification. In our book

Radical Image, we covered each tense and a bunch of other great stuff; in this book we're going to look at how we are to conform to the image of God and grow in God's grace.

Stay Balanced!

Have you ever sat on a see-saw with another person on the opposite end and tried to balance it? It's easy to ride up and down, but it is much harder to balance the board. To do it both people have to work together. Each person needs to make minor adjustments in his or her position to find the balance point. In the same way, if we want to live a stable Christian life, we need to find the biblical balance between what God does for us (His sovereignty) and our own personal responsibility. Both are clearly taught in the Bible. The board would remain level if we all stood in the middle where Christ is, but sinless perfection is impossible for us. We tip the board one way or another. Unfortunately, if either end gets too far from the centre (Christ), then the church as a whole will lose its balance and suffer.

Balancing the process of becoming like Jesus (sanctification) requires some delicate manoeuvring. It is easy to see how the see-saw can be tipped one way or the other if you look at the two extreme views of sanctification. Picking either extreme will mess up the process of being conformed to the image of God — that's why balance is so important.

One end of the see-saw emphasises the past tense or positional aspects of sanctification while overlooking the progressive, present-tense instructions. The tendency is to claim holiness and ignore the reality of sin in our personal lives and the necessity to assume responsibility for our growth. This can lead to a denial of our imperfections, and we end up having to pretend that we have it all together.

The other end of the see-saw emphasises the progressive aspects of sanctification while overlooking Scripture's more numerous references to the past-tense realities of sanctification. Some people in this group don't overlook these verses, but they treat our present position in Christ as if it were not important — as though being alive in Christ has no practical, present-day benefit. This kind of thinking usually leads to a failure to see Christians as new creations in Christ. This results in believers who struggle all their lives trying to become who they already are.

The Centre of the Board – True Humility

On either end of the see-saw we find pride. At one end of the board are those who think more highly of themselves than they ought (see Romans 12:3). They say, 'We're already holy in Christ. We don't need to concern ourselves with sin or growing towards holiness.' The other end of the board can lead to false humility. By insisting they are just sinners with desperately sick hearts, these people can claim their 'humility' while, at the same time, having an excuse to continue in sin or justifying why people still sin. But this professed humility is false. 'Look how humble I am' is a subtle form of pride.

────────────── **Check It Out!** ──────────────

Pride is like bad breath; you're the only one who doesn't know you have it!

Pride and arrogance can be our downfall. Here's a great illustration!

The World's Smartest Teenager

One fine day four people were flying in a small four-passenger plane: the pilot, a minister, and two teenagers, one of whom had just won an award for being the 'Smartest Teenager in the World.'

As they were flying along, the pilot turned to the three passengers and said, 'I've got some bad news, and I've got some worse news. The bad news is that we're out of fuel. The plane's going down and we're going to crash. The worse news is that I only have three parachutes on board.'

This meant, of course, that someone would have to go down with the plane.

The pilot continued. 'I have a wife and three children at home. I have many responsibilities. I'm sorry, but I'm going to have to take one of the parachutes.' With that, he grabbed one of the chutes and jumped out of the plane.

The Smartest Teenager in the World was next to speak. 'I'm the Smartest Teenager in the World,' he said. 'I might be the one who comes up with a cure for cancer or AIDS or solves the world's economic problems. Everyone is counting on me! The Smartest Teenager in the World grabbed the second parachute and jumped.

The minister then spoke up and said, 'Son, you take the last parachute. I've made my peace with God, and I'm willing to go down with the plane. Now take the last parachute and go.'

'Relax, Reverend,' said the other teenager. 'The Smartest Teenager in the World has just jumped out of the plane with my knapsack.'[3]

We need to stay humble, and we need to stay balanced. Ironically, the people at both extremes have a tendency towards legalism — caring about rules more than they care about people. One group has to behave as though they are completely sanctified (they believe they are). The other group emphasises obedience to the commandments of the Bible. Nobody wants to be identified as a legalist, but in many cases we have gone from negative legalism (don't do this and don't do that) to positive legalism (do this and do that). To avoid this we must understand that we are saved by faith *and* perfected by faith.

True humility is always found in Christ at the centre of the seesaw. It is confidence properly placed. We are to 'glory in Christ

Jesus, and... put no confidence in the flesh' (Philippians 3:3). Paul says, 'Let no one keep defrauding you of your prize by delighting in self-abasement' (Colossians 2:18 NASB). God is not trying to put us down. He is trying to restore a fallen humanity and build us up, and we should be building up each other as well. We are never to think we have arrived and understand everything.

Paul said, 'I am confident of this very thing, that He who began a good work in you will perfect it until the day of Christ Jesus' (Philippians 1:6 NASB). We ought to have the same confidence that the seed sown in our hearts will bear fruit, and we can present every person complete in Christ (see Colossians 1:28). If truth is the means by which we are set apart (sanctified), then faith is how truth is gathered up through thought and action. Let's look at how we respond to the truth through how we think and what we believe.

Responding to God's Truth Through Faith

There is no operating principle of life that has greater significance in our daily walk than the understanding of faith. The writer to the Hebrews says, 'Without faith it is impossible to please God' (Hebrews 11:6). Every aspect of life is shaped or determined by what we believe. First, we are saved by faith: 'It is by grace you have been saved, through faith' (Ephesians 2:8). And second, we walk or 'live by faith, not by sight' (2 Corinthians 5:7). Faith is the only means by which we relate to God.

There are three principles of faith that need to be understood and appropriated if we hope to be led by the Lord, stay in His will, and conform to His image.

1. Faith is dependent upon its object.
The question is not if you believe or how much you believe. The real question is *what* you believe, or *whom* you believe in, because everybody walks by faith. The only difference between Christian faith and non-Christian faith is the *object* of the faith.

Consider the simple action of driving. Coming to a green light at an intersection, you believe that the cross-traffic has a red light even though you can't see it — that's faith! You also believe that those who are driving on that cross-street will obey the law by stopping at the red light — that's using even more faith. Then, when you finally drive through that intersection, you exercise even more faith in mankind, the laws of our country, and the electric circuitry of the traffic lights. If you didn't have such faith, how would you approach that intersection?

'Faith is the assurance [substance] of things hoped for, the conviction [evidence] of things not seen' (Hebrews 11:1 NASB). Approaching a green light at an intersection without slowing down requires an inner assurance that there will be no collision — because if there is a collision it's going to be fatal because mum or dad will kill you if you so much as scratch the car. Boldly driving through that intersection without checking the cross-traffic puts a lot of faith on mankind, especially since you are putting your life on the line! If you have that much faith in fallen humanity, how much more faith should you have in Jesus Christ, who said, 'I am the way, and the truth, and the life' (John 14:6)?

Hebrews 13:7,8 says, 'Remember your leaders, who spoke the word of God to you. Consider the outcome of their way of life and imitate their faith. Jesus Christ is the same yesterday and today and forever.' Notice that the writer of Hebrews didn't tell his audience to imitate their leaders' *actions*, but rather, their leaders' *faith*. That's because their actions were a product of what they believed, or better, whom they believed in — God. You can't have faith in faith, because faith has no validity without an object. The 'Faith Hall of Fame' members listed in Hebrews 11 had great faith because they had a great God — and so do we! And the fact that God cannot change or lie is what makes Him and His Word the *only* legitimate object for our faith. Have you ever noticed that our faith in something grows when it has demonstrated consistency over time? God's unwavering consistency proves He is worthy of our faith.

2. How much faith we have is determined by how well we know the object of our faith.

If we know seven promises from God's Word, the best we can have is a seven-promise faith. If we know 7,000 promises from God's Word, we can potentially have a faith based on 7,000 promises. In Romans 10:17, Paul said, 'Faith comes from hearing the message, and the message is heard through the word of Christ.'

That is why faith can't be pumped up. Any attempt to step out in faith beyond that which is known to be true leads to disaster. If we make assumptions about God without checking out what the Bible says, we are setting ourselves up for disappointment and undermining our future confidence in God. We can't merely assume anything to be true; we have to *know* it to be true. A similar problem occurs when people respond to the gospel message by saying, 'Oh, I could never believe that!' Of course they could believe it. If one person can believe the truth, then any other person can do likewise. Of course, belief is a choice. Faith is something you *decide* to do, not something you *feel* like doing. It's like the story of the atheist and the Quaker.

> Once upon a time, an atheist was arguing with a Quaker about the existence of God.
> 'Did you ever see God?' asked the atheist.
> 'No,' said the Quaker.
> 'Did you ever smell God?' asked the atheist.
> 'No,' said the Quaker.
> 'Well then,' said the atheist with a big smirk on his face. 'How can you be sure there is a God?'
> The Quaker spoke in his King James English and said, 'Friend, did thou ever see thy brain?'
> 'No,' said the atheist.
> 'And did thou ever smell thy brain? the Quaker asked again.
> 'No,' said the atheist.

'Dost thou believe that thou hast any brains?' asked the Quaker once more.[4]

Every person has to decide who or what they will believe. Joshua said, 'If serving the LORD seems undesirable to you, then choose for yourselves this day whom you will serve.... But as for me and my household, we will serve the LORD' (Joshua 24:15). 'Elijah went before the people and said, "How long will you waver between two opinions? If the LORD is God, follow him; but if Baal is God, follow him"' (1 Kings 18:21). Our sanctification is totally dependent upon what we choose to believe. Every great Christian has chosen to trust in God and believe that His Word is absolute truth and the only authoritative and infallible source for life and living. The only other choice is to believe in one or more of God's created and fallen beings, including Satan and ourselves. That would be an unfortunate choice because 'the foolishness of God is wiser than man's wisdom, and the weakness of God is stronger than man's strength' (1 Corinthians 1:25).

3. The Bible presents faith as an action word.
This principle is what James is trying to get across when he says, 'What good is it, my brothers, if a man claims to have faith but has no deeds? Can such faith save him?... But someone will say, "You have faith; I have deeds." Show me your faith without deeds, and I will show you my faith by what I do' (James 2:14,18). He makes an even stronger statement later: 'A person is justified by what he [or she] does and not by faith alone' (2:24). Does that mean we aren't saved by faith and faith alone? No! We need to understand what James is trying to say. In the Bible, the English words *faith*, *trust*, and *believe* come from the same Greek noun, *pistis*, or verb, *pisteuo*. In common English usage, however, to believe in something has less personal commitment than to trust in something. It is easy to give mental assent by saying 'I believe that' and totally miss the biblical meaning of belief. Biblical faith is not just giving mental assent

to something; it also requires full reliance upon it. It's like the story about the man who fell off the cliff:

> One day a man was walking close to a steep cliff when he lost his footing and plunged over the side. As he was falling he was caught on a tree that was sticking out about halfway down the cliff. He managed to get untangled and found himself hanging from a weak limb with both hands. He looked up and saw that the cliff was almost perfectly straight, and he was a long way from the top. He looked down and it was a long, long way down to the rocky bottom.
>
> At this point the man decided that it was time to pray. He didn't pray a long, wordy prayer, he simply yelled out, 'God, if You're there, help me!'
>
> About that time he heard a voice coming from high up above that said, 'I'm here My son, have no fear.'
>
> The man was a little startled at first by God's voice, but he pleaded, 'Can You help me? Can you help me?'
>
> God replied, 'Yes, I can My son, but you have to have faith. Do you trust Me?'
>
> The man answered, 'Yes, Lord, I trust You.'
>
> God said, 'Do you really trust Me?'
>
> The man, straining to hold on replied, 'Yes, Lord, I really trust you.
>
> Then God said, 'This is what I want you to do. Let go of the limb, trust Me, and everything will be all right.'
>
> The man looked down at the rocks below, then he looked up at the steep cliff above him and yelled, 'Is there anybody else up there?'[5]

Often our lips say that we trust God but are we really relying on Him? That is why James said, 'You believe that there is one God. Good! Even the demons believe that — and shudder' (James 2:19). In other words, the demons believe there is one God, but that belief doesn't translate into trust. If we truly believe in God and choose to believe that what He says is the only absolute truth, then it should affect the way we live. For example, Jesus said, 'Blessed are those who hunger and thirst for righteousness, for they shall be satisfied' (Matthew 5:6 NASB). Do you believe that? If you do, are you hungering after righteousness?

Lately, the idea of biblical faith has been twisted by the 'name it and claim it' or 'positive confession' movement. The people within this movement advocate that we can use faith to do or accomplish anything we want. They base their teaching on passages such as Matthew 21:21,22 (NASB):

> Truly I say to you, if you have faith, and do not doubt, you shall not only do what was done to the fig tree, but even if you say to this mountain, 'Be taken up and cast into the sea,' it shall happen. And all things you ask in prayer, believing, you shall receive.

Followers of the positive confession movement rightly point out that the mountain is removed only when faith is put into operation — when we say, 'Be taken up.' That is, what you believe needs to be acted upon, which is in keeping with what James says about belief. You step over the line of biblical Christianity when you begin to think something has to happen simply because you said it. Only God can speak and bring something into existence, and we are not God. We simply cannot create reality with our mind, as New Age teachers would have us believe. As created beings, we can only respond to reality in a responsible way.

Also, we don't have the privilege or the right to determine for ourselves what it is that we are to believe. The teaching that if we believe something hard enough it will become true is not biblical. True Christianity says, 'It is true; therefore, I believe it.' Just because we believe something doesn't make it true, and our unbelief doesn't make something false. We as Christians choose to believe the truth; we don't choose what truth is.

Jesus said He is the way, the *truth*, and the life (John 14:6, emphasis added). Through our prayers and reading of God's Word, God reveals *His* truth to us. He can reveal the truth, show us the way, and give us the life we need in order to follow Him. Truth originates in heaven, and our responsibility is to believe it.

Coming Up Higher

Read

Ephesians 2:8; Hebrews 13:7,8; 2 Corinthians 5:7.

Reflect

To live a stable Christian life, we need to find the biblical balance between God's sovereignty and our responsibility.

What is positional sanctification?

What is progressive sanctification?

Do you lean more towards positional or progressive sanctification?

Explain how we are both saved by faith in Jesus' work on the cross and perfected by faith.

_____ is the means by which we are sanctified; _____ is the means by which truth is appropriated through thoughts and actions; faith is dependent upon its _____.

According to Hebrews 13:7,8 what makes Jesus Christ the only legitimate object of our faith?

Respond

Lord, I want to stand strong in You. To do that I need to set my eyes on You. I am so thankful that You are a sound object of my faith. I know that no matter what the circumstances of my life, You are faithful and You are at work conforming me into the image of Your Son, Jesus. Thank You! In Jesus' name I pray, amen.

Peace and fulfilment come from a
sincere relationship with God, and
our Lord Jesus Christ, who called us.[1]

— *Henry Blackaby*

The Power of Truth

Storing the Truth in Our Hearts

The faith that will actually change our character and also our
behaviour involves believing and putting our trust in the truth.
We need to let truth sink so deep into our hearts that our faith
is not just mental assent but something everyone can see. Paul
said, 'Let the peace of Christ rule in your hearts' (Colossians
3:15). The word *rule* means 'to act as a referee.' We are to let the
peace of Christ decide all the matters of our hearts. The question is, How do we get that truth into our hearts? The next verse
says, 'Let the word of Christ dwell in you richly as you teach
and admonish one another with all wisdom' (3:16). Although

separated in our English translations, the words *let* and *dwell* are one word in the original Greek text, and it means 'to live in, to take up one's residence in, or to make one's home among.' *What* or *who* is Paul saying should take up residence in our hearts? 'The word [Greek, *logos*] of Christ.' The truth that centres on Christ, which He embodies, is to be at the very core of our being. We are to let His peace make the call like a referee at a football game. When it comes to the matters of our hearts, we need a referee because the voices of the world, the flesh, and the devil are trying to get us to listen — and if we listen to them, they will try to gain control.

If ever we find that the battle for our mind is not very intense, it's probably because we are giving up without a fight. The need to submit to God and resist the devil (James 4:7) can't be overstated because 'the weapons we fight with are not the weapons of the world. On the contrary, they have divine power to demolish strongholds' (2 Corinthians 10:4). We need the peace of God to guard our hearts and minds (see Philippians 4:7).

Imagine that your mind is like a jug that was intended to be filled with crystal-clear water, but it got contaminated with diet soda. (Diet. It's just 'die' with a 't' on the end.) Anyway, one day you decide you want the water in the jug to be pure, but you're totally discouraged when you discover there is no way to get the terrible diet toxin out. Then you discover a bowl of crystal-clear ice cubes nearby labelled 'Word of God'. Work with me on this one, okay? There is no way you can pour the whole bowl of ice cubes into the jug at once, so you drop in one ice cube a day. At first the task seems hopeless because there is so much diet soda. Slowly, however, the daily dose of truth eventually dilutes all the colour of the toxic soda. Then finally comes the day when the diet soda can no longer be seen, smelled, or tasted, even though a remnant of it is still there. Likewise, that process of renewing our minds *will* work, provided we don't pour in a can of diet soda with every ice cube.

The Great Value of Meditation

According to Joshua 1:8, meditating on God's Word is the key to successful living: 'Do not let this Book of the Law depart from your mouth; meditate on it day and night, so that you may be careful to do everything written in it. Then you will be prosperous and successful.' The meaning of the word *prosperous* is 'to accomplish satisfactorily what is intended.' The Hebrew word for *success* refers to having wisdom that leads to wise behaviour. In the Bible, wise behaviour means a life that conforms to the character of God. To be successful or live wisely involves two things: 1) doing according to the truth of the Word of God, and 2) continual meditation on the Word, which produces that doing.

The psalmist began the book of Psalms by saying that meditation is the key to life. Here's Eugene Peterson's paraphrase from THE MESSAGE: 'How well must God like you — you don't hang out at Sin Saloon, you don't slink along Dead-End Road, you don't go to Smart-Mouth College. Instead you thrill to God's Word, you chew on Scripture day and night' (Psalm 1:1,2).

There are certain things that the blessed or happy person does not do. He or she doesn't take advice from the unrighteous: 'What partnership have righteousness and lawlessness, or what fellowship has light with darkness?' (2 Corinthians 6:14 NASB). Neither does the blessed person identify or party with sinners: 'Do not be misled: "Bad company corrupts good character"' (1 Corinthians 15:33). Nor does the blessed one mock God or His Word. Instead, we delight in the truth and meditate on it continuously. Consequently, we are like trees planted by streams of water, which yield their fruit in season and whose leaves do not wither. Whatever we do prospers (see Psalm 1:3).

Meditation in the Bible

The words *meditate* or *meditation* are found at least twenty-one times in the Old Testament, and eight of those times are in Psalm 119 alone. But the concept of meditation is mentioned in other ways throughout the Bible. For example, in Deuteronomy 6:6–9 (NASB) we read,

> These words, which I am commanding you today, shall be on your heart; and you shall teach them diligently to your sons and shall talk of them when you sit in your house and when you walk by the way and when you lie down and when you rise up. And you shall bind them as a sign on your hand and they shall be as frontals on your forehead. And you shall write them on the doorposts of your house and on your gates.

One of the most natural things we do is think and talk about what is on our hearts. If God's Word is hidden in our hearts, we will speak of it from sunrise to sunset. It will affect all that we do (hands), all that we think (frontals on forehead), all that happens in our homes (the doorposts of our houses), and all that we do publicly (the gates).

The next time you can't sleep at night because of bad circumstances, try what David did. Focus your mind on God by recalling great moments you have had with Him. Then mentally ascribe to Him His attributes. Finally, involve your whole body by raising your hands or lying prostrate before Him and singing. Fixing your eyes on Jesus, the author and finisher of your faith, will refocus your troubled mind, and singing will give greater expression and harmony to your troubled soul. Like the psalmist, you will be able to say, 'Why are you in despair, O my soul? And why are you disturbed within me? Hope in God, for I shall again praise Him, the help of my countenance, and my God' (Psalm 43:5).

The Meaning of Meditation

There are two basic words for meditation in the Old Testament. The first is *utter* or *speak*, or *muse*. Although it can be used to speak of silent musing, it seems that the basic idea of the word involves some kind of utterance — such as murmuring, or whispering, or talking to yourself. Also it is used in reference to resounding music or music that continues to sound — as if it were echoing.

The second word for meditation means to rehearse something over in one's mind. It may be done outwardly (talking) or inwardly (meditation). Meditating on God's Word helps us go beyond superficial obedience to His commands. It helps us absorb the rich meaning of what He has to say. For instance, Psalm 119:129 (NASB) says, 'Thy testimonies are wonderful; therefore my soul observes them.'

Let's take the twenty-third psalm and meditate on the first verse: 'The LORD is my shepherd, I shall not be in want.' Notice the psalmist doesn't say '*a* Lord,' he says '*the* Lord.' There is only one Lord. He is *the* Lord, and the word *Lord* is the English rendering of the divine name for God, which is YHWH (Yahweh). This sacred name for God wasn't spoken by the Hebrews; His name was considered too holy. Clearly, the psalmist was being reverent. He was saying in a sense, 'God is not my lord in the sense of being my boss; He is the almighty, everlasting God of all creation.'

What's amazing is that this Lord is our shepherd — right now. The verse doesn't say He *will be* our shepherd sometime in the future, nor *was* He our shepherd sometime in the past. He *is* at this present moment our shepherd. What an overwhelming thought that the God of Abraham, Isaac, and Jacob is *our* personal shepherd! He watches over us and leads us by quiet waters. While other sheep may win mankind's awards for beauty or performance, we have the assurance that He is *always* our shepherd and cares for us. If we should lose our way, He will leave the others to find us. What a wonderful shepherd! He will protect us from the wolves even if it costs Him His life. What more could we want?

Can you see the value of meditating upon God's Word? Psalm 23 is just one example of how God's powerful words and truths can bring blessing, comfort, and reassurance to us if we let them permeate our hearts.

Wrong Uses of Meditation

Just like faith, the object of our meditation is the big issue. Encouraging people to meditate without telling them what to meditate on can be destructive to their spiritual health. They could end up paying attention to a deceiving spirit such as those described in 1 Timothy 4:1: 'The Spirit clearly says that in later times some will abandon the faith and follow deceiving spirits and things taught by demons.' At our 'Stomping Out the Darkness' conferences, four per cent of the teens we surveyed who had trusted Christ as their Saviour also said that they had had, at one time, spirit guides. Seventy per cent said they heard voices in their minds. Deceiving spirits love it when a believer meditates on the wrong things. God wants us to select carefully what we meditate on. We never just let our mind go, and God never bypasses our mind. He works *through* it. Scripture instructs us to direct our thoughts outwardly, never inwardly, and actively, never passively. To let your mind go passive is the most dangerous thing you can do spiritually. 'Be transformed by the renewing of your mind... think so as to have sound judgement' (Romans 12:2,3 NASB).

Directing our thoughts inwards leads to nothing but morbid introspection. We're to invite God to examine us: 'Search me, O

God, and know my heart; test me and know my anxious thoughts. See if there is any offensive way in me, and lead me in the way everlasting' (Psalm 139:23,24).

The whole purpose of the meditative practices of Eastern religions is to induce a passive state of mind. In transcendental meditation, for example, you close your eyes and repeat your mantra over and over again for twenty minutes. This is supposed to help you achieve a trancelike state where your mind is put in neutral, so to speak. Eastern meditation tries to get your mind out of the way so you can get 'truth' directly. It doesn't work. In fact, it can open you to demonic forces. Also, your mind would turn to mush if you did that — and Jesus warned us about praying in vain repetitions (Matthew 6:7).

Check It Out!

Frisk every thought at the door of your mind!

How Meditation Can Change Us

Thinking the wrong thoughts can lead to despair, which some of God's favourite saints struggled with. David cried out, 'How long, O LORD? Will you forget me forever?' (Psalm 13:1). Can an omniscient God forget anything or anyone forever? No. But that is what David thinks and believes at that moment. 'How long must I wrestle with my thoughts ['take counsel in my soul,' NASB] and every day have sorrow in my heart?' (Psalm 13:2). David was depressed because he was entertaining thoughts about God that were not true. After complaining about his enemies and his circumstances, he finally looked to God. Then his thoughts became focused on Him: 'But I trust in your unfailing love; my heart rejoices in your salvation. I will sing to the LORD, for he has been good to me' (13:5,6).

The apostle Paul also suffered great hardship, but he didn't lose heart. He was imprisoned, beaten up a lot, shipwrecked, persecuted from within and without the Christian ranks, and on the run from continuous danger (2 Corinthians 11:23–27). You could knock Paul down, but he would always get up:

> We are hard pressed on every side, but not crushed; perplexed, but not in despair; persecuted, but not abandoned; struck down, but not destroyed. We always carry around in our body the death of Jesus, so that the life of Jesus may also be revealed in our body.... Therefore we do not lose heart. Though outwardly we are wasting away, yet inwardly we are being renewed day by day. For our light and momentary troubles are achieving for us an eternal glory that far outweighs them all (2 Corinthians 4:8–10,16,17).

Paul must have believed his own message, which is why he could live with such hardship. He said: 'I know what it is to be in need, and I know what it is to have plenty. I have learned the secret of being content in any and every situation, whether well fed or hungry, whether living in plenty or in want. I can do everything through him who gives me strength' (Philippians 4:12,13). Paul knew that our countenances are not shaped by the circumstances of life, but by how we perceive them. If we interpret the trials and tribulations of life correctly, they will produce character, and that is where our hope lies because the love of God has been poured into our hearts (Romans 5:3–5). In Philippians 4:8,9, Paul shares the mental focus that we must have:

> Finally, brothers, whatever is true, whatever is noble, whatever is right, whatever is pure, whatever is lovely, whatever is admirable — if anything is excellent or praiseworthy — think about such things. Whatever you have learned or received or heard from me, or seen in me — put it into practice. And the God of peace will be with you.

The word *think* in the phrase *think about such things* is the word that means 'to consider or calculate'. The NASB translates this phrase, 'let your mind dwell on these things' (4:8). Paul is not talking about superficial thinking; he is referring to the process of disciplining our minds to think truthfully, carefully, and comprehensively. This is not merely trying to remember a Bible verse when we're tempted or in trouble as if it were some magic formula. This is learning to think biblically about everything in life.

How Meditation Can Affect Our Actions

The New Testament doesn't use the term *meditate* very often, but the idea of meditation appears a lot. For example, Colossians 3:1,2 says, 'Since... you have been raised with Christ, set your hearts on things above, where Christ is seated at the right hand of God. Set your minds on things above, not on earthly things.'

Whatever we meditate on in our minds goes into our hearts and affects our actions. I remember listening to a sports pro- gramme covering the winter Olympics when East Germany was still its own country. The commentators were talking about the East German luge racers who would stop at the top of the run, close their eyes, and seem to go into some kind of meditative state. A sports psychologist explained that they were going over the whole run in their minds, every grade and turn. The first time down the run would be a learning experience, but every successive run would leave more and more of an imprint on the mind. After enough runs, the luge racers could mentally picture the entire course, and then they could prepare themselves for trying to win the gold medal on the final run.

The same thing takes place when we learn to ride a bike or drive a car, especially a vehicle with a stick-shift mechanism. After many practice attempts, the process eventually becomes more a part of you so that you can ride the bike or drive the car almost without any thought at all.

In the same way, when we continually think upon God's truth, it enters into the depths of our hearts. Whatever is borne into the depths of our beings will come out in our words and actions. 'The good man brings good things out of the good stored up in his heart, and the evil man brings evil things out of the evil stored up in his heart. For out of the overflow of his heart his mouth speaks' (Luke 6:45).

Solomon's request to God for a 'discerning heart' was literally for 'a hearing heart' — a heart that hears God's Word so he could judge the people rightly (see 1 Kings 3:9). We all have 'hearing hearts' that continually take in whatever we focus our minds on. Meditating on God's Word is simply talking to our hearts so that God's truth is instilled there and comes out in our actions.

One of the more interesting ways of getting God's thoughts into our hearts is the soliloquy, which is simply talking to ourselves. Telling yourself to 'get a grip' or 'stay cool'. Notice the psalmist does that exact thing: 'Find rest, O my soul, in God alone; my hope comes from him' (Psalm 62:5) and 'Praise the LORD, O my soul; all my inmost being, praise his holy name' (Psalm 103:1). Talking to yourself may look and sound goofy, but it's a great teacher if the truth that is spoken to the soul is from God's Word or is consistent with it.

The Objects of Our Meditation

The first object of our thoughts should be God Himself. He is the Creator, the King of kings, the Sovereign Lord of the universe. We need to think about Him until we stand in awe of His greatness. Don't get the impression that we worship God because He is an egomaniac who needs His ego stroked every Sunday morning. The idea of 'appeasing God so that He won't do bad things to us' is rooted in paganism. To worship God is to ascribe to Him His divine attributes. We do this so that our minds are programmed to know Him and His ways. Meditation on God inevitably leads us to think also of His Word, His will, and His wonderful acts. Look at what the psalmist meditated upon:

> 'On his law he meditates day and night' (Psalm 1:2).

> 'We meditate on your unfailing love' (Psalm 48:9).

> 'I will meditate on all your works' (Psalm 77:12).

> 'I meditate on your precepts' (Psalm 119:15).

> 'I will meditate on your wonders' (Psalm 119:27).

> 'I meditate on your decrees' (Psalm 119:48).

> 'I meditate on [your law] all day long' (Psalm 119:97).

> 'I meditate on your statutes' (Psalm 119:99).

> 'I... meditate on your promises' (Psalm 119:148).

> 'I meditate on all your works' (Psalm 143:5).

Beyond God and His ways, we should meditate on whatever is good. Recall Paul's words in Philippians 4:8: 'Brothers, whatever is true, whatever is noble, whatever is right, whatever is pure, whatever is lovely, whatever is admirable — if anything is excellent or praiseworthy — think about such things.' We're not saying you should deny your negative circumstances; we need to stay in touch with reality. But God tells us that our minds should not *dwell* on negative things. Yes, we need to face our problems, but we also need to focus on Christ and His truth that will set us free. When we are spiritually tired, we need to respond to the invitation, 'Come to me, all you who are weary and burdened, and I will give you rest' (Matthew 11:28). When we are fearful, we need to remember that God is present: 'Do not fear, for I am with you; do not be dismayed, for I am your God' (Isaiah 41:10).

> The guillemot is a small Arctic sea bird that lives on the rocky cliffs of the northern coastal regions. Guillemots

flock together by the thousands in a very small area. In these extremely crowded conditions, the females lay their pear-shaped eggs side by side in a long row on a narrow ledge. But what is amazing is that although the eggs all look alike, the mother bird can identify the eggs that she laid. She knows her own eggs so well that when even one of them is moved, she will find it and return it to its original location.[2]

Why should we ever fear or worry? We have an awesome God who can create a guillemot that cares for its children so well. Our heavenly Father certainly can identify us and our needs and care for us fully. 'I will strengthen you and help you; I will uphold you with my righteous right hand,' He assures us (Isaiah 41:10). And in the times when we feel guilty, we need to know that 'there is now no condemnation for those who are in Christ Jesus' (Romans 8:1).

Visualisation: Preparing for Action

Is there a place for sanctified imagination? Is there such a thing as Christian visualisation? There is nothing wrong with visualising yourself doing something in the power of the Holy Spirit, provided your thoughts are consistent with God's Word. When you're preparing to share Christ with an unsaved friend, have you ever visualised yourself doing the task in the power of the Holy Spirit? When I (Dave) was asked to visit my 92-year-old aunt, I sensed God calling me to witness to her. So I meditated on what I would say, what verses I would share. I mentally practised what the meeting would be like. That day my 92-year-old aunt received Christ as her personal Saviour. Meditating in advance can really make a difference in preparing for life. But such visualisation needs to be tempered by the truth taught in 1 Peter 1:13: 'Prepare your minds for action; be self-controlled; set your hope fully on the grace to be given you when Jesus Christ is revealed.' We prepare our minds for action.

Be careful! You will depart from reality and enter a world of fantasy if you imagine things that are not consistent with God's Word or you never do what you visualise. Remember, you are preparing your mind for action. The New Age practice of visualisation has no basis in truth because the intention of this practice is to *create* truth or reality with the mind. Those who engage in such a practice are being deceived and are deceiving others. Hope is not wishful thinking, nor does our hope lie in our own strength and attributes. Hope is the present assurance of some future good, which is based solely on the grace of God — not on people acting as their own gods.

Truth, Christ, and Ourselves

When John said that 'the Word became flesh and made his dwelling among us,' he was saying the Word of God had become man (see John 1:14). Jesus is the embodiment of the written Word. He is exactly what truth looks like. You can't separate Jesus from His Word because He *is* the Word. Everything He thought, felt, and did was true because He is the truth. If we were fully sanctified in the truth, we would think, feel, and do what Jesus did. Because we have the life and mind of Christ (1 Corinthians 2:16), the truth is within us and causes us to fall in love with God and mankind. We fall short of true Christianity if we say we know the Word of God, when it has not touched our hearts nor transformed our characters to be like Christ.

When truth is appropriated, it touches every aspect of the heart. We are emotionally transformed, and our wills are moved to action. The psalmist says, 'May my meditation be pleasing to him, as I rejoice in the LORD' (Psalm 104:34). Meditation on the Word produces thoughts that reach our emotions. If thought and feelings are joined in the heart, then any thoughts that reach the heart will touch the emotions. God's Word will not change our lives unless it changes our emotions.

Thinking Upon the Truth

Our emotions are the products of our thought lives. We are not shaped so much by the external events in life as we are by how we perceive them. Every experience is picked up by one or more of our five senses and sent to the brain (computer) to be processed by the mind (CPU). It would logically follow, then, that if what we think does not reflect truth, then what we feel does not reflect reality. For example, suppose you are waiting to hear the outcome of an important job interview. You are one of the two final candidates for a position you want very much. While you are waiting, a false rumour circulates saying that the other person got the job. Let's say you hear the rumour and believe it. How would you feel? Probably very disappointed.

In reality, however, you got the job, but your interviewers haven't had a chance to tell you yet. Suppose a friend inside the company hears the good news and calls you. When you answer the phone he says, 'Hey, congratulations!' You respond angrily, 'Why are you being so rude? You know I wanted the job, now how am I going to pay for university?' Unaware of the rumour, your friend wonders why you are upset. It's because you *think* you didn't get the job. Your feelings are a product of a lie, a false rumour. Why are you feeling angry, upset, and disappointed? You are feeling that way because of what you believed — whether it was true or not. But when you find out that you did get the job, will your feelings change? Absolutely!

There are countless thousands of young Christians who have let Satan's lies affect the way they feel about themselves and God. They don't feel saved, or they think that God doesn't love them. Why? Because wrong thoughts have been raised up against the knowledge of God. Unfortunately, just telling some people the truth will not necessarily resolve their problems. For example, a girl who had some serious problems was referred to me (Neil) for counselling. Condemning thoughts were plaguing her continuously. After listening to her for thirty minutes, I said, 'You really love Jesus, don't you?' She nodded in agreement. 'And you really love the Holy Spirit, don't you?' Again she agreed. 'But you don't even like God the Father, do you?' She broke down and cried because her beliefs about her heavenly Father were distorted. She needed God's truth to set her free.

Are you and your friends missing the great biblical truths today? Do you feel it difficult to relate to God and to talk to Him? After years of helping students, I (Neil) have discovered that the primary problem is a lack of genuine repentance along with unresolved personal and spiritual conflicts. Bitterness due to unforgiveness is the biggest hurdle for most young people to overcome.

Many teens have discovered that repenting from sin, pride, rebellion, bitterness, and deception results in a freedom that they had never experienced. When they resolved their conflicts, they were able to connect joyfully with their heavenly Father — as did the girl mentioned a moment ago.[3] Those who are free in Christ have a peace guarding their hearts and their minds. They know who they are as children of God because the Holy Spirit is bearing witness with their spirits. Before they resolved their conflicts, the Holy Spirit was being quenched — but now the Spirit of truth is bearing witness in repentant hearts.

The Place of Emotions

One of the most common results of finding freedom in Christ is that our emotions and true feelings come alive. We begin truly to love God, and His Word comes alive. Feelings are released from the subconscious to the conscious, which moves people to act in accordance with the truth that transformed their emotions. Look at the life of Christ. First, because He was 'moved with compassion' He fed the multitude (Matthew 15:32–37), healed two blind men (Matthew 20:34), cleansed the leper (Mark 1:41,42), and He forgives us all (Matthew 18:27; Mark 3:28; 1 John 2:12). Second, because the Lord was moved by anger, He overturned the tables of the moneychangers. They had turned God's house of prayer into a den of robbers (Matthew 21:12). It is important to note that He turned over the *tables*, not the moneychangers. If we are moved by anger and wish not to sin, then we should be angry as Christ was — angry at *sin*. Anger that is rooted in righteous indignation is not wrong; it moves us to take action against what is unrighteous. God works through the emotional core of our hearts to move us to repentance. We see this in 2 Corinthians 7:9,10 (NASB), where Paul said, 'I now rejoice, not that you were made sorrowful, but that you were made sorrowful to the point of repentance; for you were made sorrowful according to the will of God, in order that you might not suffer loss in anything through us. For the sorrow that is according to the will of God produces a repentance without regret.'

Many young people feel sorry about their pasts or sorry that they shared about their pasts with others. But I have never seen anyone feel sorry after he or she repented. The conviction of sin produces the sorrow that leads to repentance *without regret*. True inner peace is the result of *complete repentance*. King David is a good example. He became physically sick when he kept quiet about his sin with Bathsheba. But the hand of God pressed heavily upon him until he finally repented. Then he was able to say, 'Blessed is he whose transgressions are forgiven, whose sins are covered! Blessed is the man whose sin the LORD does not count against him and in whose spirit is no deceit' (Psalm 32:1,2). This tells us that sorrow that leads to repentance is never divorced from the truth that is within us. In Psalm 51:6, after David repented of his sin with Bathsheba, he said, 'Surely you desire truth in the inner parts; you teach me wisdom in the inmost place.'

Meditation Increases Our Faith

When we meditate on God's greatness and His love for us, we see all that He has done for us. Then we are led to place our confidence in Him. David's meditation led him to declare, 'My soul clings to you; your right hand upholds me' (Psalm 63:8). David didn't give up on God even thought the Lord allowed him to be driven into the wilderness. His soul clung to God even in the midst of difficult circumstances. The truth of God's love for him, which had been confirmed in the past, was engraved on his heart. He didn't let outward circumstances in the present erase that truth — and neither should we. David, through meditation, realised that God was upholding him. He knew he was being sustained by God's strong right hand. That's the kind of faith that allows God to work in our lives.

When we realise that God is always present and at work in our lives, life becomes different. We have the power we need to live no matter what the circumstances. We're not talking about a power that merely makes us happy, but one that gives us an inward joy that becomes our strength. Meditating on the truth prepares us for all of life's circumstances according to Proverbs 6:20–22:

> My son, keep your father's commands and do not forsake your mother's teaching. Bind them upon your heart forever; fasten them around your neck. When you walk, they will guide you; when you sleep, they will watch over you; when you awake, they will speak to you.

For instance, a lady who was critically injured in an auto accident was semiconscious for several weeks, during which time she heard careless hospital personnel refer to her as having only a short time to live. During the same time she heard other words speak to her from her inner being — words such as those in Psalm 34:4: 'I sought the LORD, and he answered me; he delivered me from all my fears.' She had memorised these words years before. In her dim awareness, she found comfort and strength in them. Eventually she recovered, and she says that the truths she meditated on were her source of hope during her battle to stay alive. Another example of the power of meditating on God's truth concerns a soldier who spent eight years in a

North Vietnam prison. He received hope and comfort from some hymns that he had sung as a child. He reconstructed 120 hymns, which gave him strength during his imprisonment.[4]

Not only can we receive comfort and strength from words we've meditated upon, we can receive correction as well. The psalmist declared, 'How can a young man keep his way pure? By living according to your word. I seek you with all my heart; do not let me stray from your commands. I have hidden your word in my heart that I might not sin against you' (Psalm 119:9–11).

Simple Methods of Meditation

Christian meditation is basically thinking on the Word of God, going over its truths in our minds repeatedly so that they finally reach our hearts, affecting our emotions and wills. But *how* should we practise meditation? Check out following helpful hints for hiding God's Word in our hearts:

1. Personalise the truth.
Place yourself or your name in the verse. For instance, Romans 5:5 says, 'God has poured out his love into our hearts.' Say to yourself, 'God has poured out his love into *my* heart.' You could also put yourself into Paul's prayer in Ephesians 3:14–19:

> For this reason *I* kneel before the Father, from whom his whole family in heaven and on earth derives its name. *I* pray that out of his glorious riches he may strengthen [*me*] with power through his Spirit in [*my*] inner being, so that Christ may dwell in [*my*] heart through faith. And *I* pray that [*I*], being rooted and established in love, may have power, together with all the saints, to grasp how wide and long and high and deep is the love of Christ, and to know this love that surpasses knowledge — that [*I*] may be filled to the measure of all the fullness of God (emphasis added).

It is too easy for us to sit outside the experiences of life and critique them without applying them to ourselves. Often when we go to church or our youth group, we critique the teaching and the worship band (or the lack of one). But we aren't supposed to sit in judgement of the message; the message is to sit in judgement of us! We're not supposed to criticise the music; we are to join together with the corporate body of Christ and worship God. We aren't supposed to study Scripture so we can tell others what to do; we are first to put Scripture to work in our own lives and then share from our hearts the truths of God's Word. Anything less is dead religion — and no one will listen to that.

2. Visualise the truth.

The Bible gives us many word pictures. What kind of mental picture comes to your mind after reading Romans 5:5: 'God has poured out his love into our hearts'? Try to picture what Jesus said in John 7:38 about the person who believes in Him: 'From his innermost being shall flow rivers of living water' (NASB).

3. Respond to the truth.

If God's Word calls for praise, then stop and praise Him. If you really want to establish truth and praise in your heart, then learn to sing in your heart. Those who are filled with the Holy Spirit and the Word of God will sing and make melodies in their hearts to the Lord (see Ephesians 5:16–20; Colossians 3:15–17). If Scripture calls for repentance and confession, then stop and fulfil the command. If it calls for obedience, then by all means decide that you will obey. James 1:22–25 talks straight about obedience:

> Do not merely listen to the word, and so deceive yourselves. Do what it says. Anyone who listens to the word but does not do what it says is like a man who looks at his face in a mirror and, after looking at himself, goes away and immediately forgets what he looks like. But the man who looks intently into the perfect law that gives free-

dom, and continues to do this, not forgetting what he has heard, but doing it — he will be blessed in what he does.

4. Let God's Word transform you.

Meditating on Scripture involves reading the Bible not just for information, but for transformation also. It is not simply a question of getting into the Word; it is a question of the Word getting into us. It is not merely getting through the Bible in a year; it is letting Bible truths get through us and lodge in our hearts. It means staying in the Word until it reaches our emotions and our wills.

5. Meditate on the Word to strengthen your relationship with the Author.

You are hearing from God. It is a basic truth of Scripture that we, as Christians, live by the Word of God. We are born again by the Word, and we grow by the Word. The Word is food for our souls. In order to grow by that food, we must take it in and digest it. Meditation is the digestive process we use to incorporate the Word into our lives. It allows us to take God's truths into our hearts, the wellspring of our lives.

Coming Up Higher

Read

Joshua 1:8; Psalm 1:1–3.

Reflect

According to Joshua 1:8, meditating on God's Word is the key to successful living. Read Psalm 1:1–3. What is the value of meditating on God's Word? How can meditation change us?

What are the five practical methods of meditation?

1. _____ the truth.

2. Visualise the _____.

3. _____ to the truth.

4. Let God's Word _____ you.

5. Meditate on the Word to strengthen your _____ with the Author.

Choose one passage from the chapter that you can focus on, then go through the five steps. Be sure to personalise what you visualise.

Respond

Lord God, I want to be faithful and go daily to Your truth for wisdom and comfort. David, Solomon, and other people in the Bible had great faith because they had a great God — and so do I! I praise You for Your greatness. Clearly, meditation on Your Word will result in a sharpened awareness and a better appreciation of Your greatness. Help me store what I learn in my mind so I can stand strong in You. Keep me in Your Word. In Jesus' name I pray, amen.

> Our significance is secured! That's the leading feature of the good news of our redemption. How liberating it is to be released from the futility of trying to get our significance apart from Christ. He has something much better for us — restoration to the Father's house as full heirs. Everything we could wish for to complete our lives is available to us in Christ — including a sense of significance beyond anything this seductive world can offer.[1]
>
> — *Joe Stowell*

3

The Power of Our Actions

One of the more popular toys that a child enjoys receiving for a birthday or Christmas present is a Slinky® — that is, if his parents can't afford a computer game. Even youth pastors like to watch the spiralling cylinder of wire snake itself down the back stairway of the church when the senior pastor isn't looking. Children, and even some senior pastors, will play with it time and again, watching it slink from one hand to the other or playing with it like a yo-yo.

Understanding Christian Growth

Christian growth is somewhat like a Slinky® that is being stretched to its limit. We cycle from one experience to another as we ascend upwards in Christian maturity. Paul revealed this cycle of growth in Colossians 1:9–12, which we just quoted. The fact that you can even begin to grow is based on the truth that God 'has qualified you to share in the inheritance of the saints in the kingdom of light.' And Paul shares how we can grow by giving us the foundational elements, which are listed in the following diagram:

The Cycle of Growth

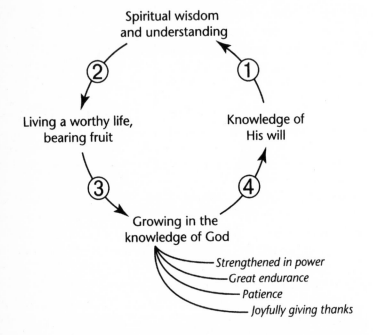

The Cycle of Growth

The process of growth begins with a knowledge of God's will, which we find in God's Word. His truth must enter our hearts for us spiritually to understand how it applies to life in all wisdom. The cycle isn't complete, however, until we choose to live according to what we understand. Living by faith requires us to exercise our will by being submissive through humble obedience. When we do, we grow in the knowledge of God, and the cycle comes full circle, back to where we started. In other words, we will receive greater knowledge as we act out the knowledge we already have.[2] The spin-offs of this growth cycle are increasing spiritual strength, endurance, patience, joy, and thankfulness, which become increasingly evident in our character.

The cycle can be blocked at any one of the four points in the diagram. We can block it at the first stage by reading the Bible as a textbook, never seeking to apply it to our lives. We would have knowledge, but no wisdom or understanding of how the Word of God applies to life.

At stage two, God's Word could penetrate our hearts and consequently convict us of sin and give us wisdom and direction for life. But the growth process would again be stopped if we never actually acted on our understanding by stepping out in faith. The usual culprit here is fear, such as fear of failure or fear of rejection. Fear of anything other than God tears down our faith. That is why we are to encourage one another, 'for God did not give us a spirit of timidity, but a spirit of power, of love and of self-discipline' (2 Timothy 1:7).

At the third stage, we grow and bear fruit when we decide to live by faith. We actually gain knowledge from our experiences. Our faith can have only one object and that is God (and His Word), but maturity gained through living causes us to understand the Word of God in a way that we didn't before. If we fail to live by faith, however, we won't bear much fruit.

Finally, we can stop the process of growth at stage four by failing to come back to the Word of God. One of the great dangers of successfully bearing fruit or experiencing victory is that we might decide to rest on our past experiences. We are tempted to think that we have arrived. That's why Paul's encouragement in Philippians 3:12–14 is so helpful:

> Not that I have already obtained all this, or have already been made perfect, but I press on to take hold of that for

which Christ Jesus took hold of me. Brothers, I do not consider myself yet to have taken hold of it. But one thing I do: Forgetting what is behind and straining towards what is ahead, I press on towards the goal to win the prize for which God has called me heavenwards in Christ Jesus.

The Paths to Change

Changing the heart begins with a change of thought or belief. When truth penetrates the heart, it touches our emotional core, motivating us to action. Look at those principles again on the chart below.

The Primary Flow

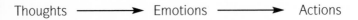

Thoughts ———————➤ Emotions ———————➤ Actions

In this chapter, we want to show that our actions influence both our thoughts and emotions. This is able to happen because these three elements are united in the heart.

Our Actions Affect Our Feelings

That an action can change how we feel was revealed early in biblical history. Remember the first brothers in the Bible, Cain and Abel? Well, they brought their offerings to God, who was pleased with Abel's offering but for some reason was not pleased with Cain's. So Cain became angry. 'Then the Lord said to Cain, "Why are you angry? And why has your countenance fallen? If you do well, will not your countenance be lifted up? And if you do not do well, sin is crouching at the door; and its desire is for you, but you must master it"' (Genesis 4:6,7 NASB).

God was saying that we don't always feel our way into good behaviour; rather, we behave our way into good feeling. If we wait until we feel like doing something, we may wait forever.

Jesus revealed the same truth in the New Testament: 'Now that you know these things, you will be blessed [happy] if you do them' (John 13:17).

─────────────────── Check It Out! ───────────────────

By acting or behaving in a certain way, we can change how we feel!

The effect of actions on feelings is plainly evident in everyday life. When we are feeling depressed, if we stop and deliberately put smiles on our faces, we find that it softens and lifts our spirits. Similarly, we have all heard of 'whistling in the dark' as an expression for keeping up our courage in the face of fear. We do it because it works. It actually affects our countenance and gives us hope.

We can 'will' ourselves out of certain moods as David did when he was depressed: 'I have trusted in Thy lovingkindness; my heart shall rejoice in Thy salvation. I will sing to the LORD, because He has dealt bountifully with me' (Psalm 13:5,6 NASB). Notice that the process began with recalling the greatness of God, and then David expresses confidence that his heart will rejoice. The rejoicing might not happen immediately, but David anticipated that rejoicing would come, even if it was some time in the future. But he did make the choice to sing as he recalled God's goodness to him.

You can do the same. When you feel down, start singing or playing a Christian CD that picks you up. That will go a long way towards changing your feelings. You can even change your feelings by simply changing your posture. If you find yourself walking around in a stooped-over slouch, the chances are you will feel like a slouch. Instead, try standing up straight, pull your shoulders back, take a deep breath, and decide to walk with confidence while holding your head up high — and see what happens to your countenance.

When we read what the Bible has to say about our emotional

life, we find that it seems to command us to feel a certain way. Many times we are commanded to rejoice and be joyful — commands that, unfortunately, are often disobeyed. There are other commandments about showing love, having peace, and not giving in to fear. All this raises a question: How are we to obey those biblical commands? If we cannot change our emotions directly, what *can* we do to change them?

Keeping in mind what we have already said about the connection between emotions and thoughts, we believe the Bible teaches that we can change our emotions by changing our thoughts. The Bible also teaches that we change our emotions by changing our actions. In other words, by acting or behaving in a certain way, we can change our emotions:

Actions Affect Emotions

Thoughts   ⟶   Emotions   ⟶   Actions

We are commanded to love one another. We are not commanded to 'like' people or feel good about them, which in some cases would be extremely difficult for us to do. We often hear people say 'I love you in the Lord,' which could imply, 'I hate your guts in the flesh!' But a love for someone or something, according to Scripture, cannot be without emotions. Because we can't directly change how we feel, these commands aren't talking about the *emotional aspects* of love, but the *actions* that proceed from genuine love. If our emotions and wills are truly connected in the depths of our hearts, then a sincere act must effect a change in our emotions. To put it simply, the doing of a loving act from our hearts also creates the emotion of love.

You may not be thinking about marriage right now, but marriage may be in the future. Husbands are to love their wives as Christ loved the church (Ephesians 5:25), and older women are to teach younger women to love their husbands (Titus 2:3,4).

Most married couples will tell you that the *emotional* aspect of loving their spouses comes and goes like the wind. What makes a marriage relationship unique is commitment, but what makes it great is the gracious act of one person loving the other whether he or she feels like it or not. And the essence of such love is meeting each other's needs. When one partner says he or she doesn't feel any love for the other person, that person is advised to honour his or her marriage vows and faithfully love the other person by meeting his or her needs. In doing so, the feelings towards the other person will follow in time.

Doing the loving thing based on God's Word will eventually connect emotionally in our hearts. That will be true if there are no unresolved conflicts caused by not speaking the truth in love or no failure to forgive from the heart. (For more about friendships, dating, true love, and sexual purity check out Neil and Dave's book *Purity Under Pressure*.)

Our Actions Affect Our Thoughts

If our actions can affect our emotions, it must be true that our actions can affect our thoughts and beliefs:

Actions Affect Thoughts

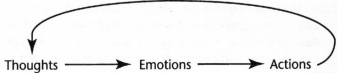

Thoughts ⟶ Emotions ⟶ Actions

Again this is seen both in human experience and in the Bible. For example, a girl told me (Neil) that she wanted to believe that there was a God, but she just couldn't get herself to do it. No amount of proof that I could offer seemed to help, so I advised her to live as though there was a God. Because she wanted to believe, she took my advice. I saw her again a year later, and I could hardly believe the change. Her decision to live like a Christian helped serve as a catalyst to actually becoming one.

If a person lives out a certain role, that role will become internalised and can bring about change to the person, including his or her thinking. For example, young girl smokers who played the emotional role of a lung cancer victim cut back their smoking more than those who were simply given information about the hazards of smoking. The Marines' promise to 'make a man out of you' is not done by intellectual study, but 'by active practice of the new role requirements.'[3] You have a better chance of becoming a mature man or woman if you act like one.

A Principle Taught in Scripture

Not only are thoughts and actions connected in certain biblical terms, they are also connected in the teachings of Scripture. After assuring us that God's divine power has granted us everything pertaining to life and godliness (2 Peter 1:3), and that we have been made a partaker of the divine nature (verse 4), Peter then shares our responsibility:

> For this very reason also, applying all diligence, in your faith supply moral excellence, and in your moral excellence, knowledge; and in your knowledge, self-control, and in your self-control, perseverance, and in your perseverance, godliness; and in your godliness, brotherly kindness, and in your brotherly kindness, love (2 Peter 1:5–7 NASB).

Faith is the foundation that leads us towards the ultimate character of love. In fact, faith is the basis for all that we are and do. If what we believe is wrong, then all that comes from us will be messed up. We can't do anything without first thinking it. Every action is preceded by a thought. That is how the central nervous system operates. We choose to believe the truth and act accordingly, which should result in right behaviour and moral excellence. Why, then, does knowledge follow moral excellence in Peter's progression towards love? Perhaps that is best illustrated by the relationship between a teenager and a parent.

Suppose a father tells his son to do something, and the teenager says, 'I don't know why I have to do that.' Does that sound familiar? The father may say, 'Trust me, I know what is best.' The rebellious son may respond, 'I'm not going to do it until you tell me why.' At that point he doesn't need an explanation, he needs to be disciplined *in love*. The father would be wise to say *in love*, 'Son, you need to do it because I asked you to do it, and when you have done it we will sit down and talk.' The point is, the *only* appropriate response to faith in God is to do it — and then you will know why. You don't have to know why in order to trust and obey, but there is a good chance that you will know why if you have been faithful. The knowledge gained from the experience of trusting and obeying leads to greater self-control, which eventually is perfected in love.

The understanding of love is borne out in our actions. Have you seen the picture of two hands put together in prayer? It's a great example of love at work:

> The famous *'Praying Hands'* picture was created by Albert Durer, who was born in Germany in 1471, the son of a Hungarian goldsmith. While Albert was studying art, he and a friend roomed together. The meager income that they earned on the side as they studied did not meet their living expenses. Albert suggested that he go to work to earn the necessary income for both of them while his friend pursued his studies. When finished, the friend would then go to work to provide support while Albert continued his studies. The friend liked the plan, but insisted that he be the first to work so Albert could continue his studies.
>
> Albert became a skilled artist and engraver. After selling a wood engraving one day, Albert announced that he was ready to begin supporting his friend as he studied. But with all the hard menial labour, his friend's hands were so swollen that he was no longer able to hold a brush, yet alone use it with skill. His career as an artist was ended.

Albert was deeply saddened by his friend's suffering. One day when he returned to their room, he heard his friend praying and saw his hands held in a reverent attitude of prayer. At that moment, Albert was inspired to create the picture of those praying hands. His friend's lost skill could never be restored, but through this picture Albert Durer felt that he could express his love and appreciation for his friend's self-sacrifice.[4]

Albert's friend didn't talk about love, he demonstrated it, and that love changed Albert's life. Jesus also demonstrated to us what love looks like:

> This is how we know what love is: Jesus Christ laid down his life for us. And we ought to lay down our lives for our brothers. If anyone has material possessions and sees his brother in need but has no pity on him, how can the love of God be in him? Dear children, let us not love with words or tongue but with actions and in truth (1 John 3:16–18).

We (Neil and Dave) have counselled hundreds of teens who said they loved the Lord, yet their lives were all messed up, and many were living in sin. Something was wrong with their faith foundation because Jesus said, 'Whoever has my commands and obeys them, he is the one who loves me' (John 14:21). On the other hand, we have worked with hundreds of young people who weren't very lovely. In some cases we had to work at loving them. Yet we are always amazed at the miracle of love that takes place in our hearts after we have done everything we can to help them. An emotional bond develops — a bond that comes by actively loving them by the grace of God.

Be Willing

The intertwining of thought and action can also be seen in the biblical teaching that truth is what a person *does*, not simply what he knows. John said, 'Whoever lives by the truth comes into the light, so that it may be seen plainly that what he has done has been done through God' (John 3:21). Living by the truth brings it into the light. The more we choose to live the truth, the more we come to know the truth. 'If we claim to have fellowship with him yet walk in the darkness, we lie and do not live by the truth' (1 John 1:6). John also said he receives great joy from knowing that his friends are 'walking in the truth' (2 John 4; 3 John 3,4).

Jesus said, 'If any man is willing to do His will, he shall *know*' (John 7:17 NASB, emphasis added). You probably won't understand the will of God if you aren't willing to do it. But if you are willing to do His will, then you will likely know what it is. That is especially true in divine guidance because God guides a moving ship. The rudder has no effect unless the ship is under way. God can't make midcourse corrections if the ship has never set sail.

Suppose the direction that God is taking you is on the other side of a closed door. You won't know what's on the other side of the door unless you are willing to *do* His will even before you *know* what it is. Why do you need to know what's on the other side of the door before you go through it? So you can decide beforehand whether or not you want to go? If God is God, He has the right to decide what is on the other side. If He doesn't have that right, then He isn't God.

We have to decide to trust God with our lives on this side of the closed door before He will let us see what is on the other side. Do we believe that the will of God is 'good, pleasing and perfect,' as Romans 12:2 tells us? According to that verse, the renewing of our minds will result in testing and proving that the will of God is indeed ideal for us.

Our Actions Affect Our Knowledge

When the Bible talks about how our actions affect our thoughts, we find that there is a big connection between knowledge and action. We rightly think of the 'fear of the Lord' as being the beginning or first principle of wisdom (Psalm 111:10; Proverbs 9:10). So we figure out that wise living begins with knowing God and being in awe of Him. But the 'fear of the Lord' is more than knowledge and awe; it also includes a practical life of displaying that awe and, therefore, is much the same as 'wisdom'. In fact, Job made this connection: 'The fear of the LORD — that is wisdom' (Job 28:28).

Both the fear of God and wisdom involves belief and behaviour, but if we live what we believe then our understanding increases. Someone wisely said, 'Do the thing you fear the most, and the death of fear is certain.' Likewise, Psalm 111:10 (NASB) begins, 'The fear of the Lord is the beginning of wisdom,' but then goes on to say, 'a good understanding have all those who do His commandments.'

─────────────── Check It Out! ───────────────

A change of heart includes both change of mind and change of action.

Our Actions Affect Our Faith

We should also listen to what James said about how works affect our faith. After declaring that Abraham's faith was at work in the act of offering Isaac, James then added, 'As a result of the works, faith was perfected' (James 2:22 NASB). Scripture clearly teaches that faith and works are related, but we often think of that relationship as flowing only one way — faith produces works. But James says the flow goes both ways. Works also affect faith. The idea is not that work adds something to an incomplete or defective faith, but rather that work fulfils, strengthens, and matures faith.[5] Because faith involves believing, we can say that when we actually exercise faith in an action, this action brings about a change in the believing aspect of our faith. Our actions may add new dimensions to our understanding of God and His work or simply strengthen the understanding we already have.

Showing Ourselves Faithful

If we want to grow in our spiritual life, we must internalise the truth of God as well as know it. Having biblical knowledge by itself does not necessarily change our lives, but when we practise God's truth, we actually gain in our knowledge and insight of His truth. A change of heart includes both change of mind and change of action. We cannot directly command our emotions, but we can choose to believe the truth and live accordingly, which increases our understanding and changes the way we feel.

Coming Up Higher

Read

Colossians 1:9–12; Psalm 13; 1 John 3:16–18.

Reflect

The apostle Paul gave us a cycle of Christian growth in Colossians 1:9–12. What are the four stages?

What can block them?

Which stage of Christian growth is the most difficult for you?

How are you searching to remove the block?

Read Psalm 13. What does David show us in his life and struggles about changing our feelings by changing our behaviour?

Write down or share a time when your good behaviour changed the way you were feeling.

1 John 3:16–18 teaches that actions affect our thoughts. What actions are commanded in these verses? What will follow if we act obediently?

Having Bible knowledge by itself doesn't necessarily change our lives, but when we practise God's truth and love Him and those around us, our knowledge and insight of His truth grow.

Respond

Lord God, thank You for Your plan of sanctification, Your plan to make me more like Your Son. Please show me where I am blocking growth in that direction and what I need to do to help growth happen. I realise that my actions are key to faith, so I'm asking for Your help. Give me strength to choose to act lovingly to my friends and family. Help me do what's right. I pray this in Jesus' name, amen.

> Legalism is conforming to a code or system of deeds and observations in the power of the flesh, hoping to gain the blessing and favour of God by such acts. Legalism invariably denies the principle of grace and exalts the pride of man.[1]
> — *Charles Swindoll*

What About God's Rules?

Christian maturity is about living a balanced and real life. Remember the see-saw in chapter one? The same delicate balance exists with the concept of freedom. Legalism and licence (unconstrained actions) sit on opposite ends of the board with our freedom in Christ at the centre. Although at first both ends of the see-saw can look reasonable, these extremes take away the joy of freedom and set us up for deception. It's important to stand by the truth:

A man was looking for a job, and he noticed that there was an opening at the local zoo. He enquired about the job and discovered that the zoo had a very unusual position they wanted filled. Apparently their gorilla had died, and until they could get a new one, they needed someone to dress up in a gorilla suit and act like a gorilla for a few days. All he had to do was just sit, eat, and sleep. His identity would be kept secret, of course. Thanks to a very fine gorilla suit, no one would be the wiser.

The zoo offered good pay for the job, so the man decided to do it. He tried on the suit and sure enough, he looked like a gorilla. They led him to the cage; he took a position at the back of the cage and pretended to sleep. But after a while he got tired of sitting, so he walked around a little bit, jumped up and down and tried a few gorilla noises. The people who were watching him seemed really to like that. When he moved or jumped around they would clap or cheer and throw him peanuts. And the man loved peanuts. So he jumped around some more and tried to climb a tree. That seemed to get the crowd excited. They threw more peanuts. Playing to the crowd, he grabbed a vine and swung from one side of the cage to the other. The people loved it and threw more peanuts.

'Wow, this is great!' he thought. He swung higher and the crowd grew bigger. He continued to swing on the vine, getting higher and higher — and then all of a sudden, the vine broke! He swung up and out of the cage, landing in the lion's cage that was next door. He panicked. There was a huge lion not twenty feet away, and it looked very hungry. So the man in the gorilla suit started jumping up and down, screaming and yelling, 'Help, help! Get me out of here! I'm not a real gorilla! I'm a man in a gorilla suit! Heeelllppp!' The lion quickly pounced on the man, held him down and said, 'Will you *shut up!* You're going to get us both fired!'[2]

The two men working at the zoo were as phony as phony gets. Unfortunately, our youth groups and churches have some phonies, too. Some wear the legalism costume and others a licence suit. People love to watch the tricks they do; they cheer and clap. Eventually, however, the deception is revealed when a crisis in the lives of phonies causes them to falter or fail spiritually. Legalism and licence rob us of our freedom in Christ.

In Romans 6:1–11, Paul identifies us with Christ in His death, burial, and resurrection. He says in verses 5 and 7, 'If we have been united with [Christ Jesus]... we will certainly be united with him in his resurrection.... Anyone who has died has been freed from sin.'

Every Christian has died with Christ and is freed from sin. Paul adds in Galatians 5:1,2: 'It is for freedom that Christ has set us free. Stand firm, then, and do not let yourselves be burdened again by a yoke of slavery. Mark my words! I, Paul, tell you that if you let yourselves be circumcised, Christ will be of no value to you at all.' In other words, don't go back to the law. If you claim you are already free in Christ, but you are wearing the legalism suit or have failed to live a responsible, biblically based life, you are at one of the ends of the see-saw. You are sacrificing your freedom in Christ.

Living Free in Christ

Every Christian is a child of God and is free in Christ. But how many people live like they are? We estimate that only ten per cent of Bible-believing, teenage Christians are living free, productive lives. What a tragedy! Being alive and free in Christ is the birthright of *every child* of God. Those who are liberated know who they are in Christ, bear fruit, and have satisfying prayer and devotional lives. Sure they have problems, but they resolve them in Christ. We don't believe in instant maturity; we know it will take us the rest of our lives to renew our minds and conform to God's image. We know we will never achieve perfection in our relatively short lifespan, but our focus should still be on becoming like Christ. Yet there is a major difference between the issues that make up freedom and those that make up growth.

If a person isn't experiencing freedom in Christ, then he or she is stymied in Christian growth. People like this go from book to book, youth pastor to youth pastor, and counsellor to counsellor, trying to get unstuck. But when their eyes open to the truth about who they are in Christ and they have resolved their personal and spiritual conflicts, watch them grow!

Making the Right Choice

While I (Dave) was in Alaska, I had an opportunity to see some of the sights around Anchorage. We saw a moose, ate halibut, and had a great time. One of the more serious sights was the huge mud flats. The youth pastor that was showing me around said that people die there every year because they think the warning signs don't apply to them. One story that comes from the area has a particular sobering effect. There is a place called the 'Turn-Again Arms'. This particular area has one of the fastest tide rates in the world. The tide rushes in and out at about ten feet per minute. The water is so cold that if you got caught in it you would die within a few moments. When the tide is out, there is a huge flat area of mud. It looks like a great place to ride off-road vehicles. But this area isn't just mud. It is also glacial silt. When the tide rushes out, the water that is left settles quickly. When it settles, it leaves air pockets, and those air pockets form vacuums. You never know where they are, and they are never in the same place twice. If you step in one of them, it will suck you in and you can't get out. It's not exactly like quicksand. It's more like superglue as it locks you in.

> In the summer of 1991, a couple who had just got married decided to spend their honeymoon in this part of Alaska. They went out riding ATVs and decided to ride around on one particular mud flat. The bride's vehicle stalled, and she jumped off to see what the problem was. She jumped into one of these areas of glacial silt and sank in up to her knees. As she struggled to get out, she sank

to her thighs. Her husband rode up on his ATV, and she warned him not to get off his vehicle. People on the road above them saw what was happening and called for help, yelling at the man not to get off his vehicle. Within moments the fire department arrived and tried to blast her out of the mud flat by using water hoses. It didn't work. Then they brought in an army helicopter and attached a harness about her waist. As the helicopter pulled up her legs dislocated. They knew that if they pulled any more they would have ripped her legs from her body. They tried to put a wet suit around her, thinking that when the tides came in, it would keep her warm. But they could only get the wet suit around part of her body. When the tides came in she died while her husband helplessly watched.

That tragic story illustrates what sin is like. It looks good. It looks inviting. You see it and just want to get out there and have fun. But it turns out to be glacial silt. It sucks you in and ultimately ends up taking your life.[3]

Paul says 'sin shall not be your master, because you are not under law, but under grace' (Romans 6:14). We can choose to live as though we are still under the law and rob ourselves of the freedom Christ purchased for us on the cross. We can also go to the other extreme, licence, which Paul warns against in Galatians 5:13: 'You, my brothers, were called to be free. But do not use your freedom to indulge the sinful nature [flesh]; rather, serve one another in love.' Both legalism and licence lead to bondage that can be taken care of only through repentance and faith in God.

Imagine walking down a narrow mountain road. On one side is a steep drop-off. It is too steep to climb down, and too far for you to jump. On the other side of the road is an intense forest fire. Behind you is a roaring lion (and it's not a guy in a lion suit this time). The lion is hungry and seeking someone to devour. Ahead of you is a church. Which way would you go? One option would be to jump off the cliff. You would experience an initial sense of freedom and perhaps exhilaration from the free-fall. But there are serious consequences to that choice — like the sudden stop at the end that would do more than mess up your hair. That is the nature of licence, or being licentious (a total disregard for rules and regulations). Licence is counterfeit freedom. The 'free' sex that was so popular in the sixties and seventies came with a staggering price tag. Instead of sexual freedom, people got caught in sexual bondage and were infected with venereal diseases that tore up many homes and marriages. Some choices have consequences.

True freedom doesn't just lie in a person's right to make choices. It comes by making responsible choices based on the truth of God's Word. This makes the freedom that Christ purchased for us on the cross a living reality. The tempter has a field day with those who choose the licence end of the see-saw. He whispers, 'Go ahead and do it. You know you want to. Everybody else does it.' Temptations always look good, or nobody would ever give in. When was the last time you were tempted to eat spinach?

Another option on the narrow mountain road is to turn into the forest fire, which represents legalism. The result is just as disastrous: 'Burn, baby, burn.' The accuser has a field day with those who choose the legalism end of the see-saw. He tells them they'll never measure up and that God is disappointed in them.

Temptation and accusation are two sides of the coin Satan flips in his relentless pursuit of our defeat. We are truly liberated in Christ when we walk the balance between legalism and licence. All the sanctuary we need is right in front of us, but it isn't the church building. The only sanctuary we have in this present time is our position in Christ. In Him, we are safe and secure: 'Now the Lord is the Spirit, and where the Spirit of the Lord is, there is freedom' (2 Corinthians 3:17).

The Curse of Legalism

Paul wrote, 'All who rely on observing the law are under a curse, for it is written: "Cursed is everyone who does not continue to do everything written in the Book of the Law." Clearly no one is justified before God by the law, because, "The righteous will live by faith"' (Galatians 3:10,11). It's not God's law that is a curse, but legalism. With such clear statements from Scripture, why are we still struggling with legalism after 2,000 years of church history?

Check It Out!

We are not saved by how we behave, but by how we believe!

Those who choose to relate to God purely on the basis of law will indeed be cursed. These are the perfectionists who believe they can be good enough and do enough to keep the law. But they can't: 'Whoever keeps the whole law and yet stumbles at just one point is guilty of breaking all of it' (James 2:10). No one is perfect enough to adhere 100 per cent to the law.

Paul said, 'If a law had been given that could impart life, then righteousness would certainly have come by the law' (Galatians 3:21). But the law is powerless to give life. Telling someone that what he or she is doing is wrong does not give that person the power to stop doing it. Thankfully, we are not saved by how we behave, but by how we believe. If we are saved by our actions, nobody would have any hope because none of us can do enough; it is Jesus who saves us — not the law.

Even more devastating for the legalist is the truth taught in Romans 7:5: 'When we were controlled by the sinful nature, the sinful passions aroused by the law were at work in our bodies, so that we bore fruit for death.' The law actually has the capacity to stimulate our desire to do what it prohibits. Paul continues, 'But sin, seizing the opportunity afforded by the commandment, produced in me every kind of covetous desire'

(Romans 7:8). If you don't think that is true, watch what happens when your parents tell your little brother that he can't go into your room. The moment they say, 'You *can't* go into your brother's room,' where will he want to go? Into your room! He probably didn't even want to go there until they told him he couldn't. Why is forbidden fruit seemingly the most desirable? Such a question caused Paul to ask, 'What shall we say, then? Is the law sin? Certainly not!' (Romans 7:7).

What Is God's Law?

Now that we are in Christ and no longer under the law, how do we relate to the law? To answer that, we need to understand what the law of God is. The term *law* in the Bible is often associated with specific commands, especially the commands of the Old Testament Mosaic Law (for example, Romans 2:20–27). But the concept of God's law is much broader. The Hebrew word *torah*, which is the basic term for 'law' in the Old Testament, is related to the Hebrew verb *hora*, meaning 'to direct, to teach, to instruct in.'[4] It is similar in meaning to the New Testament Greek word for law, which is *nomos*. Its main meaning is not 'command', but 'instruction'. So this word came to be used not only for specific laws, but for the entire Word of God and its record of God's dealings with His people.

The essential element in the biblical concept of the law is seen in the explanation of *torah* as 'that which points the way for the faithful Israelite and for the community of Israel. Not merely the laws of the Pentateuch (the first five books of the Old Testament) provide guidance; the entire story of God's dealings with mankind and with Israel points the way.'[5] Thus the term *law* can refer to entire sections of Scripture and to Scripture as a whole, including both God's commandments and His gracious promises. Such is the case in Matthew 5:17, where Jesus said He came not to abolish the law, but to fulfil it.

The law of God may be said to be the expression of His will that stems from His holy character. Even as there are physical laws by which the physical world is structured, so also are there personal and moral spheres of God's creation governed by His moral and spiritual laws (expressions of His holy nature). With that in mind, it is interesting that the apostle Paul never spoke of God's law in the plural, but only in the singular. In the final analysis, all laws are expressions of the unified moral character of God. For Israel, God's law took the form of the written Scriptures; for the Gentiles, it was the law 'written on their hearts' (Romans 2:15). But there is 'only one Lawgiver' for all people (see James 4:12).

To encounter God's law is to come in contact with God. Scripture says that all people are aware of that law in some way: 'Since the creation of the world God's invisible qualities — his eternal power and divine nature — have been clearly seen, being understood from what has been made, so that men are without excuse' (Romans 1:20). Many people don't acknowledge God. They see the created order of the universe, but they depersonalise God because an impersonal god doesn't have to be served. So they worship the creation rather than the Creator. Thus, the sinful mind is said to be hostile to God. 'It does not submit to God's law, nor can it do so. Those controlled by the sinful nature cannot please God' (Romans 8:7,8).

As the expression of the moral structure of the universe, God's law is designed for the good of His creatures. Just as the laws of physics permit our world and universe to run smoothly, the law of God is designed for the well-being of His creatures. His commandments are not restrictive; rather, they are protective and have our best interests at heart. Remember the signs that warned the couple not to go out on the glacial silt? The authorities didn't post the signs to ruin the couple's fun, but to protect them from the dangers of the silt. It is God's revelation that brings true life, peace, well-being, and fullness of joy. *God's moral laws are designed for the blessing of His people.* The Christian life is often termed *the Way*, and God's laws are the rules of the way.

As we have seen, God's law is seen in all of His dealings with His people — in His historical actions as well as His words, in

His gracious promises as well as His commandments. The imperatives (commands) as well as the gracious promises of salvation are God's truth — truth that He uses to sanctify and transform His people. Paul describes the Mosaic Law as 'the embodiment of knowledge and truth' (Romans 2:20). The psalmist delighted in God's law, declaring, 'Your law is true' (Psalm 119:142).

The commands of Scripture are part of the truth that sanctifies. They are part of the truth that brings life, as opposed to the lies that express unreality and lead to suffering and death. The commands in Scripture are expressions of God's holy love for us. We are to impress His commands on our hearts and teach them to others (see Deuteronomy 6:6–9).

Not only do God's commands express His love for us, they are also the sum of what it means for us to live in love towards God and our neighbours: 'Love is the fulfilment of the law' (Romans 13:10); 'the entire law is summed up in a single command: "Love your neighbour as yourself"' (Galatians 5:14). God's laws are the moral base of the universe that rightly relates and binds us to God and the rest of humanity in the perfect way of truth and life. His laws provide the essential aspects of the truth that we must focus on to have a transformed life.

Our Relationship to God's Law

Because God's laws are the moral principles of the universe, we can say that all moral creatures relate to these laws. In the Old Testament, believers as well as unbelievers were subject to the overarching principle that following God's laws led to life, and disobeying them led to misery and death. Believers 'in Christ', however, relate to that law principle in a radically different way from people without Christ. The latter stand before the law in themselves, as sinners and, consequently, lawbreakers. They live under the condemnation of the law and the penalty of death. But believers 'in Christ' have the same relationship to the law that Christ has.

We Are Free

What is Christ's relationship to the law? Scripture says that the law has reached its fulfilment in Christ, meaning that God's righteous principles for life all point to Christ and are fully realised in Him.[6]

--------------------- Check It Out! ---------------------

Jesus is the 'Terminator!' of the law.

Paul's statement that 'Christ is the end of the law' (Romans 10:4) expresses a single idea. The word 'end' (Greek, *telos*) means 'fulfilment', 'goal', or 'termination'. Jesus is the 'Terminator!' of the law. I bet you never thought of Jesus as the 'terminator' before, but He is. It would be best, however, if we understood *a combination* of all these meanings. Christ as the fulfilment of the law is also its goal; that is, the law looked forward to Him. And as we will see shortly, Christ also brought an 'end' to the time when God's people lived under the law like children under a tutor (Galatians 3:24).

To speak of Christ as the fulfilment or goal of the law simply means that the complete significance of the law has been attained in Him. This may be summed up in two main points. First, the law as a means of punishing lawbreakers is perfectly realised in Christ's sacrifice for our sins at the cross. Christ took the penalty of lawbreaking; He 'redeemed us from the curse of the law by becoming a curse for us' (Galatians 3:13). Christ satisfied the just requirements of the law. Second, the law as the expression of God's will was perfectly realised in Christ, who always acted in obedience to His Father's will. All of the righteousness expressed in commands and ceremonial ordinances pointed to their goal in Christ. He is the righteousness of God incarnate.

Christ as the fulfilment or end of the law clearly brings the believer 'in Him' into a radically new relationship to the law. As believers 'in Christ', Scripture describes us as no longer living 'under law', but being free from the law (see Romans 6:14,15;

Galatians 3:23–25; 5:18; Romans 7:6; Galatians 4:8,9; 5:1–4; Colossians 2:20. That's a lot of verses; why don't you take a minute and look some up?) These descriptions of the believer and the law do not mean we no longer have any relationship with God's law. They do, however, describe a freedom from the law that is absolutely vital to understand so we can live and grow as God intends.

We Are Responsible

The fact that the believer in Christ is free from the law's condemnation and custodial control does not mean that he or she has no relation whatsoever to the biblical law. Our liberty as Christians doesn't mean we are against the law. It makes us free to be what we were created to be, free to do what we know in our hearts we should do. But this kind of freedom is known only in relation to God, and relation to God cannot be in exclusion of His righteous law. Horatius Bonar said:

> Our new relationship to the law is that of Christ Himself to it. It is that of men who have met all its claims, exhausted its penalties, satisfied its demands, magnified it, and made it honourable. For our faith in God's testimony to Christ's surety-obedience has made us one with Him.... His feelings towards the law ought to be our feelings.... And does not he say, 'I delight to do Thy will, O my God; Thy Law is within my heart' (Psalm 40:8).[7]

Keeping the law before coming to Christ would be unnatural because we were dead in our trespasses and sins and were by nature children of wrath (Ephesians 2:1–3). We simply could not do it. But now that we are in Christ, living according to the righteous standards of the law by the Holy Spirit's power is the natural — or actually supernatural — thing to do. God's desire for His people is true life, and that life is lived according to His moral and spiritual laws. Sanctification and growth in holiness is, in reality, growth in conformity with God's laws.

In the sanctification process God sets before us His ways and calls us to use our minds to see them, our emotions to love them, and our wills to live them. The expressions of God's laws are thus God's aid in helping us becoming more like Jesus, living out His pattern for holiness and true life.

———————————— Check It Out! ————————————

The grace of God is not a licence to sin; it is a power enabling us to live righteous lives.

Instead of telling people to live under the 'yoke of the law,' or the Old Testament Mosaic Law, Jesus invited them to 'take my yoke upon you and learn from me' (Matthew 11:29). 'The Gospel does not command us to do anything in order to obtain life, but it bids us live by that which another has done; and the knowledge of its life-giving truth is not labour but rest — rest of soul — rest which is the root of all true labour; for in receiving Christ we do not work in order to rest, but we rest in order to work.'[8] The law for the believer in Christ is no longer the Mosaic Law, but Christ's law (1 Corinthians 9:21; Galatians 6:2), which is described by James as the 'perfect law' and 'royal law' (2:8). The grace of God is not a licence to sin; it is a power enabling us to live righteous lives.

The righteous standards of the law of Christ are expressed both in the example of His life here on earth as well as in His teachings. We are to walk as He walked, following His example (see 1 John 2:6; Romans 15:2–5; 1 Corinthians 11:1; 1 Peter 2:21). We are also to obey everything that He commanded (Matthew 28:19,20; see also John 14:15,21; 1 John 2:3–5; 3:21,22,24; 5:3). His teachings were not limited to the time span of His earthly ministry; they were also the teachings of the apostles who followed Him. In fact, the apostles' teachings were really those of our Lord (see John 14:26; 16:13; Revelation 3:7). While the teachings of Jesus and His disciples may be the most direct expression of Christ's law, in reality, *all* of Scripture is involved. Though we are no longer directly under the old Mosaic Law, the righteousness of that law is taken up in the law of Christ.

Ultimately all Scripture is the revelation of Christ and His righteousness — sometimes directly, sometimes indirectly, and sometimes in the form of temporary institutions and cere-monies or shadows. Living in Christ as the fulfilment of the law must encompass the careful study of the entire Bible. 'All Scripture... is useful for teaching, rebuking, correcting and train-ing in righteousness, so that the man of God may be thoroughly equipped for every good work' (2 Timothy 3:16,17).

To determine if commands given to believers *before* Christ apply to believers *in* Christ, we must consider the plain com-mands of Jesus and His apostles along with the fundamental moral principles found throughout Scripture. Today's believers also have the help of the indwelling Spirit, who leads and guides them in applying the objective commands of Scripture.

―――――――――――― Check It Out! ――――――――――――

It is not what we do that determines who we are; it is who we are that determines what we do.

As Christians, we are free from the law and yet obligated to keep the commandments of the 'law of Christ.' Christ's fulfil-ment of the law has brought a new kind of obedience for the person who is 'in Him'. Law-keeping is the result of a relation-ship with Christ, not the means to gain such a relationship. Our total relation to the law is now 'in Christ'. Rules without a rela-tionship lead to rebellion, but those who are rightly related to God will gladly live out His will. This means that our law-keeping is done from our position in Christ.

Divine Empowerment

Sanctification is working out the righteousness that is ours because of who we are in Christ. The law itself has no power to sanctify. Thus, keeping the law itself is not the means of our sanctification. Remember, it is not what we do that determines who we are, it is who we are that determines what we do. Sanctification is applying the finished work of Christ in our lives through the power of the Holy Spirit. We stand against the unrighteousness of this world by clothing ourselves with Christ (Romans 13:14; Galatians 3:27).

The power to overcome sin and live out the righteousness of Christ's law comes from the Holy Spirit. 'Live by the Spirit,' Paul said, 'and you will not gratify the desires of the sinful nature' (Galatians 5:16). The righteous requirements of the law are met by those who live 'according to the Spirit' (Romans 8:4). And the 'fruit of the Spirit' is the righteous fulfilment of the law (Galatians 5:22,23). Again, the power to live according to Christ's law comes only through the Spirit as He lives Christ's life (which was victorious over all sin) in and through us.

An Obedience Compelled by Love

I (Neil) was once asked on a national radio programme, 'If you could tell our audience only one truth, what would you tell them? What one thing would you want them to know most?' I paused for about a microsecond and then said, 'Your heavenly Father loves you, and He loves you far more than you could ever humanly hope for.' John 3:16 gives us some idea of the extent of that love: 'God so loved the world that he gave his one and only Son, that whoever believes in him shall not perish but have eternal life.' The love of God, not fear, is the single most powerful motivation in life: 'There is no fear in love. But perfect love drives out fear, because fear has to do with punishment. The one who fears is not made perfect in love' (1 John 4:18).

Motivating God's people by fear or laying down the law without grace is a blatant denial of the true gospel. Love becomes an even greater motive for New Testament believers. They can look back at Christ's complete fulfilment of the law on their behalf and their adoption as free children into the family of God. It was Christ's death and resurrection — and all that it meant — that made Paul a new creature who no longer lived 'under law' but was adopted into God's family as an adult son with God's Spirit living in him. That's what led Paul to say, 'Christ's love compels us' (2 Corinthians 5:14).

He First Loved Us
Love has its source only in God, and it is God's love that enables the believer to love: 'We love because he first loved us' (1 John 4:19). It is God's love that moves us to obey the law of Christ. We are reminded in John 14:15, 'If you love me, you will obey what I command.' Love is the essence of law-keeping, as Jesus demonstrated when He washed the feet of His disciples. Then He said 'My command is this: Love each other as I have loved you' (John 15:12). Paul said, 'The entire law is summed up in a single command: "Love your neighbour as yourself"' (Galatians 5:14).

The Benefits of God's Law

In addition to all the blessings that are ours because of His love and grace, God has made possible a way for us to make the great truths of salvation real in our lives. He has given us His moral laws of life so that we might have abundant life and grow towards fullness of life. The commands of the law of Christ are part of the truth God uses to transform our lives and bring increasing sanctification or holiness to us. We must never look at these commands as restrictions; rather, they are as aspects of truth designed to help us have true freedom and joy.

Coming Up Higher

Read

Galatians 3:13; 3:21.

Reflect

The extremes of legalism and licence sit on opposite ends of the see-saw. We are to be balanced and stay free in Christ. What happens if we say there is no such thing as freedom and no freedom from our past?

What happens if we ignore the principles of the law?

How in balance are you right now?

How is legalism a curse?

Why is the law powerless to give life?

Why doesn't telling someone what they are doing wrong give them the power to stop doing it?

Respond

Almighty God, I thank You for what I've realised about Your law. I thank You that Christ has already met all of the law's demands. I ask that You would enable me to allow Christ's righteousness to be worked out in my life so that I might be conformed to the image of my Saviour and be filled with His love. I ask You, Holy Spirit, to help me live according to Christ's law as You live in and through me. I pray this in Jesus' name, amen.

The Gospels show that Jesus quickly established intimacy with the people he met. Whether talking with a woman at a well, a religious leader in a garden, or a fisherman by a lake, he cut instantly to the heart of the matter, and after a few brief lines of conversation these people revealed to Jesus their innermost secrets. People of his day tended to keep rabbis and 'holy men' at a respectful distance, but Jesus drew out something else, a hunger so deep that people crowded around him just to touch his clothes.[1]

— *Philip Yancey*

5

Abiding in Christ: The Source of Holiness

Some people just want to learn facts about Jesus, but don't you want to get right next to Him and know what He's thinking? Don't you want to care deeply about the things He cares about and love the way He loves? You want to abide in Him! Trying as best as you can to live the Christian life will bear little fruit because apart from Christ you can do nothing. Only by God's grace can you live the Christian life. Only by abiding in Christ can God be seen in your life. If you know all the principles of the Bible but don't have godly character, then you are only a 'resounding gong or a clanging cymbal' that is without love (see 1 Corinthians 13:1).

Becoming like Jesus (progressive sanctification) is a super-natural work. Clearly the victory over sin and death through

Christ's crucifixion and resurrection is God's, not ours. Only God can redeem us from the power of sin, set us free from our pasts, and make us new creations in Christ. Even though we have become partakers of the divine nature owing to Christ's presence in our lives, we still need to be dependent upon God to supply the power to conform us to His image. Becoming a Christian does not mean we have more power in and of ourselves. It means we are inwardly connected to the only source of power that is able to overcome the laws of sin and death — the law of the Spirit of life in Christ Jesus (Romans 8:2). That we are tempted to misunderstand this truth, or perhaps unconsciously forget it in our attempt to grow as believers, is seen in Paul's sharp question to the Galatians: 'Are you so foolish? After beginning with the Spirit, are you now trying to attain your goal by human effort?' (Galatians 3:3).

Christ's Strength or Yours?

One of the greatest temptations we face is to stop being dependent upon God and start relying on our own intellect and resources. No matter how hard we try in the flesh to be like Jesus, we will never be able to live righteously without the Holy Spirit. The power to live the Christian life comes from dependence, not self-determination. It's like the young girl who tried to control her excitement when she saw a movie star. She was trying to act cool and in control, but she ended up looking foolish.

The girl who was from the Midwest made a trip to Hollywood, California to see the sights and hopefully to catch a glimpse of a real movie star.

> One afternoon, she visited Beverly Hills and went into an ice cream shop to get an ice cream cone. She put in her order and then suddenly realised that the person standing next to her at the counter was none other than Leonardo DeCaprio. She couldn't believe it! Her heart leapt. But she tried to keep her composure. She didn't want to act like

an ignorant hillbilly. She didn't want to embarrass herself in front of someone like Leonardo. So she tried not to stare or show any emotion. She paid the cashier, turned, and walked calmly out of the store.

When she got outside, she took a deep breath and suddenly realised she had walked out of the store without her ice cream cone. Oh no! She must have left it on the counter. Now she was going to have to go back in and get her ice cream in front of Leonardo DeCaprio. She just couldn't do that!

So she decided to wait outside the store until he had left the counter. When she noticed he was no longer there, she walked back into the store to retrieve her ice cream cone. But when she got to the counter, she felt a tap on her shoulder from behind. She turned around and... *it was Leonardo DeCaprio!*

Flashing his famous smile, he said, 'Miss, if you're looking for your ice cream cone... you put it in your purse.'[2]

Her efforts to make herself look cool went down like the Titanic! In the same way, if we try in our own strength to live the Christian life we will sink as well. As long as we think we can live the Christian life by ourselves, we will fail miserably. Wisdom says, 'Trust in the Lord with all your heart and lean not on your own understanding; in all your ways acknowledge him, and he will make your paths straight' (Proverbs 3:5,6).

Luke 2:52 gives us an idea of what true Christian growth looks like: 'Jesus grew in wisdom and stature, and in favour with God and men.' Jesus' growth was perfectly balanced spiritually, mentally, physically, and socially. Many Christian authors have endeavoured to help us know that kind of growth by writing about dating, sexual purity, prayer, and other personal disciplines. But even with all these resources available, many young Christians aren't seeing much fruit in their lives. Why?

Each discipline named in the chart on the following page is like a spoke in a large Christian wheel. Even though the spokes

Personal Disciplines

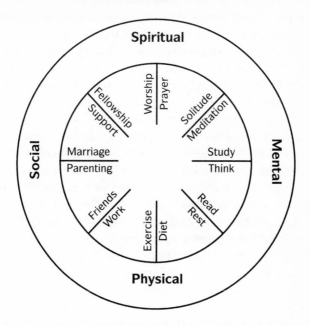

are related to the hub of the wheel, they may not be connected in a living, dynamic, dependent way. The result is a subtle form of Christian behaviouralism that sounds something like this: 'You shouldn't do that; you should do this. That is not the best way to do that; here is a better way to do it.' And we dutifully respond, 'Okay, I'll try my best.' The result is a 'try harder' lifestyle: 'You're not trying hard enough. If you try harder, maybe your Christianity will work!'

The result? Guilt. Condemnation. Defeat. Instead of being called into freedom, we are being driven into disillusionment. The farther we are from the hub, the harder we try — until something snaps. We are trying to fulfil the Bible's commands in our own strength.

Those people who are the closest to the hub are sweet-spirited and gentle, the kind of people we like to hang around with.

They seem to love others and bear fruit with little effort. They are living testimonies of the beatitudes (Matthew 5:3–12). Those people farthest from the hub are judgemental and legalistic. They can tell you with biblical accuracy how a Christian should behave. They know what is right and what is wrong. They have captured the letter of the law which kills, instead of the Spirit who gives life (2 Corinthians 3:6). They are like the men in this old story.

> According to an ancient legend, a man became lost in his travels and wandered into a bed of quicksand.
> Confucius saw the man's predicament and said, 'It is evident that men should stay out of places such as this.'
> Next, Buddha observed the situation and said, 'Let that man's plight be a lesson to the rest of the world.'
> Then Mohammed came by and said to the sinking man, 'Alas, it is the will of Allah.'
> Finally, Jesus appeared on the scene and said, 'Take My hand, brother. I will save you.'[3]

Those closest to the hub say 'take my hand,' and those outside the hub just give advice.

People who distance themselves from the hub have few or no deep and meaningful relationships. Everything remains on the surface. Any effort to break through the barriers to get to their inner selves will be resisted. Their insecurity results in complete withdrawal and passivity, or they become controllers. They are threatened by the idea of being transparent and are terrified that someone may find out what is really going on inside.

Most of these legalistic people have never had bonding relationships. They are not experiencing freedom in Christ; they have made themselves victims. Unless they are set free in Christ, they will continue their cycle of abuse. Many books have been written to help such people, yet some authors neglect to explain the right order in which to solve a person's problems.

Where Changed Behaviour Begins

Some of the Bible's practical instructions are in Paul's epistles (the second half of each letter is the applicational portion of his teaching). If you were only concerned about what to do about something, then you would probably address only those passages. Yet we cannot approach the Christian life by looking only at the practical applications. The first half of Paul's letters to the churches form a necessary foundation; they establish us in Christ. Not until we establish ourselves in the truths about being complete in Christ can we begin to apply what we find in the second half of Paul's epistles. People who try to behave as children of God will produce little fruit if they have no understanding of who they are *in* Christ or how to *live by* the Spirit's power.

Years ago in a small Midwestern town, one man's job was to watch the railroad crossing. When a train approached at night he was to wave a lantern to warn those driving on the narrow road that a train was approaching and to stop until it passed by.

One particular night the train was coming down the tracks as usual, and the man took his place to warn any oncoming cars. He could see a car in the distance approaching the railroad tracks so he began to wave his lantern in the moonlit sky. The car continued to come so the man waved the lantern ever more briskly. The train was only seconds away from the crossing. The car was not even slowing down. The man could not believe it, so he waved the lantern even harder. Still the car came. The car was almost to the track and the train was about to pass. The man could not stand in the middle of the road any longer. Again he frantically waved his lantern, and the car continued to come at full speed. Finally, the man jumped out of the way as the car sped by and was hit by the train. Thankfully no one was hurt, but the car was wrecked.

At the investigation, the grief-stricken man explained

to the authorities how he tried to warn the oncoming vehicle but it would not stop. The officer in charge said to the man at the crossing, 'Sir, you waved your lantern — but you forgot to light it.'[4]

How to wave the lantern is the application, the second half of the epistles. The flame, who we are in Christ, is the first half of the epistles. It doesn't do any good to know how to swing a lantern if it isn't lit. We have told many struggling teenagers to forget temporarily about trying to fix their relationships with parents, or boyfriends, or girlfriends. They were so torn up on the inside that they couldn't get along with their pets, much less anyone else! The problem is internal and can be solved by learning to believe and speak the truth in love. We have seen parent and child conflicts resolved when families focus on their relationships with Christ. When family members are rightly related to God, they are free, and they're capable of dealing with their other problems. We've never seen family resolutions work when that order is turned around. We spend too much time trying to change behaviour and not enough time trying to change what we believe about God and ourselves.

'As [a man] thinks in his heart, so is he' (Proverbs 23:7 NKJV). What people are on the outside is a reflection of what they are on the inside. If their beliefs are wrong, their behaviour will also be wrong. Before people can change, they must first be established alive and free in Christ (connected to the hub) so they know who they are as children of God. *Then* all those good instructional books on how to change behaviour will be effective. *Then* all those studies on family systems and role relationships will work. People can't live out the law of Christ without the life of Christ. The personal disciplines diagram should look like that on the following page.

There is nothing wrong with programmes that are designed to help Christians change their behaviour, improve their relationships, or make their families stronger as long as Christ is at the centre. Trouble starts when our confidence and dependence

Personal Christ-Centred Disciplines

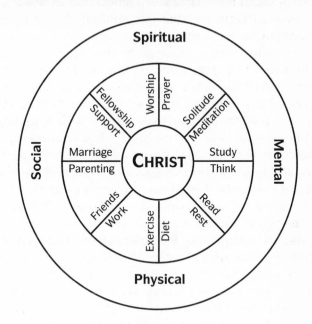

upon God gets shifted to confidence and dependence upon the programme itself. Instead of searching for God, we search for better programmes or techniques. As a result, we burn ourselves out trying to bear fruit.

Jesus tells us how our heavenly Father is glorified: 'This is to my Father's glory, that you bear much fruit, showing yourselves to be my disciples' (John 15:8). Many people miss the point. They think, 'I have to bear fruit!' No, Jesus said we have to *abide in Him* (verses 4–7). If we abide (live) in Him, we will bear fruit; bearing fruit is the evidence that we are abiding in Christ. If we are living in Christ, then any programme will work. If we try to live the Christian life in our own strength, no programme will work. Of course, when we abide in Christ, a good programme will bear more fruit than a bad programme.

Ask yourself: How much of what I do in my personal life and

relationships is based on laws or principles that call for obedience? Then ask yourself: How much of what I do is based on my spiritual life in Christ? It is your spiritual foundation that causes you to walk by faith according to what God said is true. It is this base that you live by the power of the Holy Spirit so you don't carry out the desires of the flesh. The first is a law principle; the second is grace.

God, Our Power Source

Scripture repeatedly teaches us that sanctification in our daily lives is possible only through the power of God. We are to abide in Christ, for without Him we can do nothing (John 15:4–9). It is no longer we who live, but Christ who lives in us (Galatians 2:20). The Christian life is one of walking by the Spirit and being filled or controlled by Him (see Galatians 5:16; Ephesians 5:18). We are what we are and do what we do for God only by His grace working in us (1 Corinthians 15:10).

Yet what do these statements really mean? How do they become real in our daily lives at school and at home? What does it mean to 'abide in Christ' or 'walk by faith' in the 'power of the Holy Spirit' so that true growth in holiness can take place?

Abiding in Christ

Progress in the Christian life is attained by *staying connected* with Christ through faith. This thought is expressed in a variety of ways:

- As you therefore have received Christ Jesus the Lord, so walk *in Him*, having been firmly rooted and now being built up *in Him* and established in your faith, just as you were instructed (Colossians 2:6,7 NASB, emphasis added).
- I no longer live, but Christ lives in me. The life I live in the body, I live by faith *in the Son of God* (Galatians 2:20, emphasis added).

- Be strong *in the Lord* and in his mighty power (Ephesians 6:10, emphasis added).
- *Clothe yourselves with the Lord Jesus Christ*, and do not think about how to gratify the desires of the sinful nature (Romans 13:14, emphasis added).
- Whatever you do, whether in word or deed, *do it all in the name of the Lord Jesus* (Colossians 3:17, emphasis added; see also 1 Peter 3:16 — our behaviour is to be *in Christ*).

It is clear from these verses that our lives, strengths, and all our activities as believers are to be related to Christ (connected to the hub). They are to flow out of our being in union with Christ. This truth could not be made clearer than it is in Jesus' statement about the necessity of abiding in Him: 'Abide in Me, and I in you. As the branch cannot bear fruit of itself, unless it abides in the vine, so neither can you, unless you abide in Me.... For apart from Me you can do nothing' (John 15:4,5 NASB). The Greek word translated *abide*[5] also means 'remain or continue.' But in the Gospel of John, in the context of a relationship with Christ, it denotes more than a static relationship. Paul's statements about being 'in Christ' and having 'Christ in us' are expanded upon in John's concept of 'abiding in', which expresses a dynamic, intimate union with that person.[6]

What this all-embracing concept means in our relationship to Christ is seen in the relationship between the Father and Christ. Even as we abide in Christ and He in us, so do the Son and the Father abide in each other. The result of Christ abiding in His Father is that everything He says and does manifests the character of the Father. Jesus said, 'If I do not do the works of My Father, do not believe Me; but if I do them... believe the works, that you may know and understand that the Father is in Me, and I in the Father' (John 10:37,38 NASB). In John 14:10 (NASB), He added, 'The words that I say to you I do not speak on My own initiative, but the Father abiding in Me does His works.' Christ expressed the words and deeds of the Father because He lived in obedience to Him (see John 5:19,20; 14:31).

We have the same kind of relationship with Christ that Christ has with the Father. We abide in Christ, and Christ abides in us. Through this mutual abiding, Christ conveys His life to us so that our lives display His character as we trust and obey Him.

Scripture reveals that abiding in Christ involves two basic practices: First, it means that we nourish ourselves through faith in all that Christ is to us; and second, it means that we follow Him in obedience to His commands. In a very real sense we are back to the simple concepts of 'trust' and 'obey'.

Receiving Christ by Faith

Abiding in Christ means first to receive His life and saving work into our own lives through faith. In a vivid statement Jesus said, 'He who eats My flesh and drinks My blood abides in Me, and I in him' (John 6:56 NASB). Jesus is not talking about literal eating and drinking, but, as is clear from an earlier statement, He is talking about receiving Him and His work through faith. In this verse, eating is the same as believing: 'I am the bread of life; he who comes to Me shall not hunger, and he who believes in Me shall never thirst' (verse 35 NASB). In the spiritual life, hunger and thirst are satisfied by coming to Christ or believing in Him.

Abiding in Christ is receiving by faith all that Christ is for us. In Him we are rightly related to God as His children. We are alive with His victorious eternal life. We are, in Paul's words, 'blessed... with every spiritual blessing in the heavenly places in Christ' (Ephesians 1:3 NASB).

Sometimes we don't feel spiritually blessed; we feel more like the parakeet Max Lucado talks about. He tells the story of a woman who had a parakeet named Chippie. She loved Chippie because he was such a happy little song bird. Chippie's constant chirping just seemed to brighten her day.

> One day, the woman was cleaning the bottom of Chippie's cage with a vacuum cleaner when the telephone rang. She reached for the telephone without

removing the nozzle of the vacuum cleaner from the cage, which was a mistake. The vacuum cleaner nozzle got pointed in the direction of poor little Chippie, and he was suddenly sucked up into the machine.

When the woman looked back at the cage and realised what had happened, she was horrified. She dropped the telephone, turned off the vacuum cleaner and ripped open the dust bag to get to her little bird. Chippie was a real mess, but he was still alive. She raced to the kitchen sink and turned the water full force on Chippie. The more she tried to wash him, the worse he looked, so she took him to the bathroom and started drying Chippie with her hair dryer — full force and high heat. Finally, she got the bird dry and put back in his cage.

Several days later, a friend called and asked how Chippie was doing.

'He's alive,' she said, 'but he just sits in his cage and stares out into space. And,' she added thoughtfully, 'Chippie doesn't sing much anymore.'[7]

We have all felt like Chippie from time to time, ruffled and worn out, but to abide in Christ means to consider all the blessings God has given and meditate on them. We need to appropriate them to our lives through faith. Abiding in Christ is the equivalent of letting His words live in us: 'If you abide in Me, and My words abide in you...' (John 15:7 NASB; see also John 8:31 and 1 John 2:24 regarding abiding in His words). And as we think about abiding in Christ's words, we must remember that *He is the Word incarnate*. Abiding in Christ's words doesn't simply mean that we intellectually think about truth. Rather, it means we personally relate to Him as the way, the truth, and the life. Through that personal relationship we come to know Him who is the truth.

Obeying Christ's Commands

When Jesus said He abided in His Father, He was saying that He lived in total obedience to Him. Likewise, for us to abide in Christ means that we live in obedience to our Lord. This second aspect of abiding in Christ was suggested by Jesus Himself when He said that His words were to abide in us (see John 15:7). They are so to lodge in our minds and hearts that they will direct our actions in a life of conformity to Christ — the fruit that inevitably results when a person (a branch) is abiding in the vine (see John 15:1–8).

Christ makes it clear that obedience is an aspect of abiding when He says, 'Abide in My love. If you keep My commandments, you will abide in My love; just as I have kept My Father's commandments, and abide in His love' (John 15:9,10 NASB). Keeping Jesus' commands includes walking His pattern of life. This means showing the same kind of love He showed. Jesus said, 'A new commandment I give to you, that you love one another, even as I have loved you' (John 13:34). 'A pupil [or disciple] is not above his teacher; but every one, after he has been fully trained, will be like his teacher' (Luke 6:40 NASB). John adds, 'The one who says he abides in Him ought himself to walk in the same manner as He walked' (1 John 2:6 NASB).

Living in union with Christ, which is essential for growth in holiness, involves *our constant receiving of supernatural life* from the vine and *our determination to follow Christ* in our daily walks. Jesus' illustration of the vine and the branches makes this absolutely clear. Reading this passage about fruit-bearing, we subtly hear and focus on an imperative to bear fruit. Elsewhere in Scripture, we see this fruit described in terms of our moral and ethical behaviour. But before we can bear fruit, Jesus tells us first to abide in Him, abide in His love. Just as a branch bears fruit by abiding in the vine, so we are able to live out Scripture's commands by nourishing ourselves in Christ's life.

The Priority in Abiding in Christ

That our nourishment from Christ precedes our ability to obey is seen in Jesus' command to love one another (John 15:12,17). But we cannot show this love unless we are abiding in God's love or continuing in the love we have received: 'We love because he first loved us' (1 John 4:19). It is futile to attempt to love other people unless we first nourish ourselves daily by receiving afresh God's love for us. Only as we receive God's love for us and respond in love can we obey His commandments. Our obedience is possible only as a result of the love we have for Christ: 'If you love me, you will obey what I command' (John 14:15; see also verse 21).

Conforming to the image of God is a long, steady process of internal change as we abide in Christ. People do not change overnight, nor can they be forced to do so. Abiding in Christ is being yoked to the gentle Jesus (Matthew 11:29). Servants of Christ who minister to others know that. Like Christ, they show great patience and gentleness. We grow as believers by focusing on Christ and abiding in Him by faith so that His life is lived in us. We lay hold of Him as our total salvation — past, present, and future. He not only rescued us from sin and death, but He continues to save us, conforming us to His righteousness as we follow His pattern of life in obedience.

Coming Up Higher

Read

Luke 2:52; Proverbs 23:7; John 15.

Reflect

Christian maturity is Christlike character. It's not just trying harder to live the Christian life. Only by God's grace can we live our Christian faith. What does Luke 2:52 teach us about true Christian growth?

What parts of our lives need to be in balance for true growth to take place?

What does Proverbs 23:7 teach us?

Before people can change, they must first become established in their freedom in Christ so they know who they are as children of God. Read John 15:4–7. What is the key to the passage — bearing fruit or abiding?

How have you been tempted to focus on fruit-bearing rather than the more important issue of abiding?

For us to abide in Christ means to obey the Lord's commands. This means showing the kind of love He showed. What can you do today at home, at school, or at work, to show Christ's love to someone?

What needs to be removed for you to love others the way Jesus loves them?

Respond

Almighty God, it's a real temptation for me to stop being dependent on You and, instead, to rely on my own talents and resources to live the Christian life. Please keep teaching me how to live by the Spirit's power, how to abide in You, and how to walk by faith so that I can grow in holiness. I thank You, God, for the gift of Your Son and the power of Your Spirit so that I can be sanctified and bear fruit for Your kingdom. In Jesus' name, amen.

6

Live under the Holy Spirit's control. Obey every leading of the Holy Spirit. Know that this will defeat any fleshly or carnal inclination you may have. Believe that this will result in Jesus' life being reproduced in you.[1]

— *Jack Hayford*

Filled with the Spirit: The Power of Holiness

A young pilot who was flying in bad weather found himself in a difficult situation when the weather changed for the worse. He couldn't see a thing because of the fog. He had to put his total trust in his aeroplane's instruments. He had never had to fly with just the instruments before; it was a totally new experience for him. He was a little nervous to say the least. The ink was still wet on the certificate verifying that he was qualified for instrument flying.

He wasn't worried about the flying, however. Rather, he was concerned about being able to land. His destination was a crowded metropolitan airport that he wasn't familiar with. He would be in radio contact within minutes. Until then, he was alone with his thoughts.

Flying alone with no visibility, he was aware how easy it would be to panic. Twice he reached for the radio to broadcast, 'Mayday!' Instead, he forced himself to go over the words of his instructor again and again. His instructor had practically forced him to memorise the rule book. He didn't care for it at the time, but now he was thankful.

Finally the voice of the air traffic controller was heard. Trying not to sound apprehensive, the young pilot asked for landing instructions. 'I'm going to put you in a holding pattern,' the controller responded.

Great! thought the pilot. However, he knew that his safe landing was in the hands of a person he couldn't see. He had to draw upon his previous instruction and training, and trust the guidance of the air traffic controller. The words of an old hymn, 'Trust and obey, for there's no other way,' took on new meaning. Aware that this was no time for pride, he informed the controller, 'this is not a seasoned pro up here. I would appreciate any help you can give me.'

'You got it!' he heard back.

For the next forty-five minutes, the controller gently guided the pilot through the blinding fog. Heading and altitude corrections came periodically. The young pilot realised the controller was guiding him around obstacles and away from potential collisions. With the words of the rule book firmly placed in his mind and the instructions from the controller, he finally landed safely. During the ordeal, the controller assumed that the instructions of the flight manual were understood by the young pilot. His guidance could only be based on that. Such is the case with the Holy Spirit, who guides us through the maze of life with the knowledge of God's will established in our minds.[2]

We were given the assurance of divine guidance when Jesus said, 'When He, the Spirit of truth, comes, He will guide you into all the truth' (John 16:13 NASB). Jesus is the truth, and the Holy Spirit is the agent of truth that sanctifies us. *It is the Holy Spirit who empowers us* to lay hold of all that Christ is for us and work it into us. In one of his letters, Paul said that the Corinthian believers were a 'letter from Christ [that is, authored by Christ]... written not with ink but with the Spirit of the living God... on tablets of human hearts' (2 Corinthians 3:3). It is by the Spirit that Christ lives and demonstrates His life in us. The Spirit dwells in our hearts and comes as the 'Spirit of life' — the one who 'gives life' (see Romans 8:2; 2 Corinthians 3:6). He is also the power that enables us to live righteously. The fullness of the Spirit's ministry is well summed up in Ezekiel's promise of His coming: 'I will give you a new heart and put a new spirit [living power] in you.... I will put my Spirit in you and move you to follow my decrees and be careful to keep my laws' (Ezekiel 36:26,27).

We are to focus on Christ but live by the dynamic of the Spirit. Our focus is empowered and directed by the Spirit. Every aspect of the Christian life is performed by the Spirit. In addition to living by the Spirit, we love by the Spirit (Romans 15:30; Colossians 1:8); are sanctified by the Spirit (Romans 15:16; 1 Corinthians 6:11; 2 Thessalonians 2:13); pray by the Spirit (Ephesians 6:18; see also Romans 8:26); hope by the power of the Spirit (Romans 15:13); by the Spirit put to death the deeds of the body (Romans 8:13). We are also led by the Spirit (Romans 8:14; Galatians 5:18); worship in the Spirit (Philippians 3:3); are strengthened by the Spirit (Ephesians 3:16); walk by and according to the Spirit (Romans 8:4; Galatians 5:17,18); are taught by the Spirit (1 Corinthians 2:13; 1 John 2:20,27); produce good fruit by the Spirit (Galatians 5:22,23).

Many more of the Spirit's activities in the life of the believer could be listed, but these are sufficient to show that Christian growth is accomplished only by the Spirit. It is absolutely necessary for us to be rightly related to Him and sensitive to His leading. Scripture gives us four commands about our relationship with the Spirit. Two are positive: 'walk by the Spirit' (Galatians 5:16 NASB); 'be filled with the Spirit' (Ephesians 5:18). Two are negative: 'do not grieve the Holy Spirit' (Ephesians 4:30); 'do not quench the Spirit' (1 Thessalonians 5:19). These commands are related; all are instructive about how we can enjoy a right relationship with the Spirit.

Walking by the Spirit

In Galatians 5:16 (NASB), Paul exhorts us to 'walk by the Spirit.' The Greek word translated *walk* literally means 'to go about, to walk around.' Life is pictured as a 'way' on which a person journeys. How people live or conduct their lives is considered to be the way they walk. This word picture appears frequently in the Old Testament, probably because the nomadic lifestyle was so common in the ancient world. Life for those people meant being on the move. Thus, 'to walk' means to live or conduct life.[3]

According to the Bible, a godly person lives as if he or she were always before God. God told Abraham, 'I am God Almighty; walk before me and be blameless' (Genesis 17:1). Walking before God means devotion to Him that is expressed in obedience (as seen in God's commands to Abraham to be blameless). It also results in blessings; God turns His face in grace toward the person who walks before Him. The psalmist rejoiced that he was granted the privilege to 'walk before God in the light of life' (Psalm 56:13; see also Genesis 48:15).

─────────────── Check It Out! ───────────────

Spiritual walking must have power and direction. We walk by the Spirit's power and direction.

The Bible calls the believer to walk in a certain way of life — so much so that in the New Testament times, Christians were known as 'followers of the Way' (see Acts 9:2; 22:4). We are called to a supernatural walk. Formerly we 'walked according to the course of this world, according to the prince of the power of the air' (Ephesians 2:2 NASB); 'according to the flesh' (Romans 8:4 NASB); 'like mere men' (1 Corinthians 3:3); and 'in the darkness' (1 John 1:6; 2:11). Now we are to walk in Christ (Colossians 2:6); 'in the light' (1 John 1:7); 'as children of light' (Ephesians 5:8); 'according to love' (Romans 14:15 NASB); 'in the same manner as [Jesus] walked' (1 John 2:6); and 'according to the Spirit' (Romans 8:4).

This walk is possible only as we obey the command to walk by the Spirit. Only the Spirit can overcome the tendencies of the flesh (or the characteristics of the old walk): 'Walk by the Spirit, and you will not carry out the desire of the flesh. For the flesh sets its desire against the Spirit, and the Spirit against the flesh' (Galatians 5:16, 17 NASB). We cannot put down the ways of the flesh by our own wisdom or willpower. Only the Spirit of God is capable of doing that. Our task is to walk continually — every moment — by the power and direction of the Spirit.

Just as in physical walking, spiritual walking must have power and direction, which we get through the Holy Spirit. The Spirit enables our spiritual walk because He makes us alive with the victorious life of Christ. He also provides direction: 'Since we live by the Spirit, let us keep in step with the Spirit' (Galatians 5:25). By the life given through the indwelling Spirit, we are called to walk in harmony with the Spirit, who is continually at work leading and directing our lives (Galatians 5:18; see also Romans 8:13,14). The result of this new walk is that we bear the fruit of the Spirit: love, joy, peace, patience, kindness, goodness, faithfulness, gentleness and self-control (Galatians 5:22,23). These are the manifestations of the life of Christ in us.

Inhibiting the Work of the Spirit

Living or walking by the Spirit means living in intimate fellowship with Him. But our ability to grieve the Spirit tells us that sin can hinder our fellowship (see Ephesians 4:30). As we saw earlier, Paul's first negative command about our relationship

with the Spirit is that we 'do not grieve the Holy Spirit of God.'
In that verse, the Greek word for *grieve* has the general meaning
of physical and emotional pain. What causes grief or pain to the
Spirit? The context reveals that we grieve the Holy Spirit when
we say things that tear down other believers instead of building
them up. What else grieves the Holy Spirit? In a general sense,
Isaiah 63:9,10 tells us that the answer is *sin*: 'In his love and
mercy he redeemed them; he lifted them up and carried them
all the days of old. Yet they rebelled and grieved his Holy Spirit.'
Sin is not only the breaking of God's law, it is also the wound-
ing of His heart. It places a barrier between us and the Spirit of
God, who not only indwells us but is also God's seal, the stamp
of His holy character on us (see Ephesians 1:13,14; 4:30).

Sin also stifles the Spirit's ministry in our lives and through
us to others. This is clear in Paul's second negative command:
'Do not quench the Spirit' (1 Thessalonians 5:19 NASB). In the
Bible, the Spirit's dynamic activity in us is sometimes symbol-
ised by fire; thus the NIV translates 1 Thessalonians 5:19: 'Do not
put out the Spirit's fire.' Just as fire can be extinguished by with-
holding fuel or dousing it with water, so also can we stifle the
Spirit's ministry in our lives by refusing to heed His direction or
by rejecting His ministry from others.

Paul suggested in 1 Thessalonians 5:19 that the believers were
in some way quenching the Spirit by limiting the exercise of the
spiritual gift of prophecy (and perhaps other gifts as well). But
the exhortation certainly has broader application to any sin
that disallows the Spirit's dynamic activity to be manifest in us.
'The Spirit's fire is quenched whenever His presence is ignored
and His promptings are suppressed and rejected, or the fervour
which He kindles in the heart is dampened by unspiritual attitudes, criticisms, or actions.'[4]

Walking by the Spirit, then, requires that we be sensitive to
sin in our lives. We need to walk in the light so our sins can
become exposed — not only our wrong actions, but also our
selfish desires and all fleshly thoughts. Scripture says,
'Everything that does not come from faith is sin' (Romans

14:23). John says, 'Everything in the world — the cravings of sinful man, the lust of his eyes and the boasting of what he has and does — comes not from the Father but from the world' (1 John 2:16). *The thoughts and actions of our lives are either related to the Father, or they have their source in our fallen world.*

Walking by the Spirit means renouncing all forms of worldliness, including all human wisdom (1 Corinthians 1:20 – 2:5), all human standards (1 Corinthians 2:14,15), and all human righteousness (Philippians 3:9). Walking by the Spirit entails a growing awareness of sin and even asking God to search our hearts and let us know if there are any hurtful ways in us (see Psalm 139:23,24 NASB).

Whenever sin is hindering the Spirit's ministry in us, we must deal with that sin in a biblical way:

1. *Repentance and confession* (1 John 1:9). We need to agree openly with God that we have sinned, and we need to turn from our sinful ways.
2. *Recognising and receiving God's gracious forgiveness* on the basis that Christ's work on the cross satisfied the penalty for our sins. The apostle John said that God is 'faithful and just and will forgive us our sins and purify us from all unrighteousness' (1 John 1:9). This is possible on the basis of the good news — the gospel. Christ has already made perfect satisfaction (propitiation) for our sins. We are simply to apply what He has already done (1 John 2:1,2). If we fail to claim that truth, we will be defeated by sin and unmotivated to pursue walking in the Spirit. That's not how God wants us to feel. He cares for us and is for us (Romans 8:31), even though He requires us to acknowledge our sin.

Confessing and turning from our sins renews a right relationship with Jesus. Our sins will be washed away. There's a story of a woman who visited her priest and told him that when she prays, she sees Jesus in a vision:

'He appears to me as real as you are standing here right now, Father,' said the woman. 'And he speaks to me. He tells me that he loves me and wants to be with me. Do you think I'm crazy?'

'Not at all,' replied the priest. 'But to make sure it is really Jesus who is visiting you, I want you to ask him a question when he appears to you again. Ask him to tell you the sins that I confessed to him in confession. Then come back and tell me what he said.'

A few days later the woman returned.

'Did you have another vision of Jesus?' the priest inquired of her.

'Yes, I did, Father,' she replied.

'And did you ask him to tell you the sins that I confessed while I was in confession?'

'Yes, I did,' the woman answered.

'And what did he tell you?' asked the priest expectantly.

'He said "I forgot."'[5]

God doesn't really forget things but He does choose not to hold them against us (Isaiah 43:25). He sees us through the sacrifice and character of Jesus.

Being Filled with the Spirit

The Meaning of Being Filled
Obeying the commands that tell us to avoid that which hinders the Spirit's ministry is vital for walking or living by the Spirit. But equally important — if not more — is Paul's positive command, 'Be filled with the Spirit' (Ephesians 5:18).

To be filled with something means to be 'completely controlled and stamped'[6] by its power and yielded to it. For example, some people who tried to throw Jesus off a cliff were 'filled with rage' (Luke 4:28,29 NASB). A person can be 'filled with jealousy' (Acts 5:17), 'filled with comfort' (2 Corinthians 7:4 NASB), or filled with wisdom and understanding (Colossians 1:9).

To be 'filled with the Spirit' means to let the Spirit who lives in us manifest Himself so that His presence fills us and controls all of our thoughts and actions. This fullness of the Spirit sometimes refers to special displays for particular situations; for example, the disciples were 'filled with the Holy Spirit' and spoke in tongues at Pentecost (Acts 2:4). Later, in the face of persecution, the disciples were emboldened to witness when they were filled with the Spirit (see Acts 4:8,31).

Check It Out!

Let the Spirit who lives in us manifest Himself so that His presence fills us and controls all of our thoughts and actions.

In Ephesians 5:18, however, Paul is talking about a filling of the Spirit that is an *abiding characteristic* of a person's life (see Acts 6:3). Stephen and Barnabas were such people; both were full of faith and the Holy Spirit (Acts 6:5; 11:22–24). When Paul said we are to be 'filled with the Spirit,' he wrote in the present tense, indicating that we are to let our lives be continually controlled by the Spirit. Instead of being under the influence of wine and other things that lead to trouble (Ephesians 5:8–18), we are to let the Spirit have His way in us so that our lives will manifest the character of Christ.

We make room for the Spirit's filling by emptying ourselves of self-interest and self-sufficiency. Notice that when the disciples were caught in a storm in the middle of the night, Jesus 'came to them, walking on the sea; and He intended to pass by them' (Mark 6:48 NASB). Jesus will pass by the self-sufficient. If we want to row by ourselves against the storms of life, He will let us do so until our arms fall off. Only those who are dependent upon the Lord will be helped. The Spirit can fill only what is empty.

Using the biblical truth that we reap what we sow, Paul said, 'The one who sows to his own flesh shall from the flesh reap corruption, but the one who sows to the Spirit shall from the Spirit reap eternal life' (Galatians 6:8 NASB; see also 2 Corinthians 9:6). We have a choice of living for our own selfish satisfaction with all of its works or we can give our lives over to the control of the Spirit.

Paul expressed that very thought in Romans 8:5: 'Those who are according to the flesh set their minds on the things of the flesh, but those who are according to the Spirit, the things of the Spirit' (NASB). Paul was simply describing two people: the unbeliever, whose whole existence is lived in the flesh (independent from God; in bondage to sin), and the believer, who exists in the realm of the Spirit. But Paul's description also teaches us what it means to live by the Spirit.

When we set our minds on something, it means more than simply thinking a certain way. It means to make something an absorbing interest that involves our minds, affections, and purposes. It means to have our *total* existence bent towards something. If we want to grow in the Spirit, we must continually have our minds set on 'the things of the Spirit' or, as the Jerusalem Bible says, 'spiritual things.' That's what Paul was talking about when he said we are to set our minds 'on things above, not on earthly things' (Colossians 3:2).

The Means to Being Filled
Three disciplines of the Christian walk are especially related to our lives in the Spirit. If we want to be filled with the Spirit, we must be people of prayer, students of the Word, and active in the church. Let's see how all that works.

One ministry of the Holy Spirit is that He *testifies* that we are children of God (Romans 8:16). It is the Spirit who leads us, as God's children, to cry, '*Abba*, Father' to God (Romans 8:15; Galatians 4:6). We have access to God because we are His children. We also have access to the Father through the Holy Spirit. What does this access look like?

> During the war between the American states, a young soldier in the Union Army lost his older brother and his

father in the battle of Gettysburg. The soldier decided to go to Washington, D.C. to see President Lincoln to ask for an exemption from military service so that he could go back and help his sister and mother with the spring planting on the farm. When he arrived in Washington, after having received leave from the military to go and plead his case, he went to the White House, approached the front gate and asked to see the president.

The guard on duty told him, 'You can't see the president, young man! Don't you know there's a war going on? The president is a very busy man! Now go away, son! Get back out there on the battle lines where you belong!'

So the young soldier left, very disheartened, and was sitting on a little park bench not far from the White House when a little boy came up to him. The lad said, 'Soldier, you look unhappy. What's wrong?' The soldier looked at the little boy and began to spill his heart to him. He told of his father and his brother being killed in the war and of the desperate situation at home. He explained that his mother and sister had no one to help them with the farm. The little boy listened and said, 'I can help you, soldier.' He took the soldier by the hand and led him back to the front gate of the White House. Apparently the guard didn't notice them because they weren't stopped. They walked straight to the front door of the White House and walked right in. After they got inside, they walked right past generals and high-ranking officials, and no one said a word. The soldier couldn't understand this. Why didn't anyone try to stop them?

Finally, they reached the Oval Office where the president was working — and the little boy didn't even knock on the door. He just walked right in and led the soldier in with him. There behind the desk were Abraham Lincoln and his secretary of state looking over battle plans that were laid out on his desk.

The president looked at the boy and then at the soldier

and said, 'Good afternoon, Todd. Can you introduce me to your friend?'

And Todd Lincoln, the son of the president, said, 'Daddy, this soldier needs to talk to you.'

The soldier pleaded his case before Mr Lincoln, and right then and there he received the exemption that he desired.[7]

We can come into God's presence. Just like Todd could come into the president's office at any time, we can come before God's throne at any time. The Spirit helps pray for us so that our prayers may be more effective (Romans 8:26,27). In fact, life in the Spirit is a life of unceasing prayer (1 Thessalonians 5:17). When the apostle Paul tells us to be 'strong in the Lord and his mighty power' by putting on the full armour of God, notice that his final exhortation is that we pray: '*Pray* in the Spirit on all occasions with all kinds of *prayers* and requests. With this in mind, be alert and always keep on *praying* for all the saints. *Pray* also for me' (Ephesians 6:18,19 emphasis added). Prayer has an important part in paying attention to the things of the Spirit.

Being filled with the Spirit is also the same as being filled with God's Word. The command 'be filled with the Spirit' in Ephesians 5:18 is parallel to Paul's command in Colossians 3:16, 'Let the word of Christ dwell in you richly.' (See the similarity of effects in the verses that follow.) Notice that after both commands, Paul lists the results of obeying the command (filled with the Spirit, singing psalms, hymns and spiritual songs with gratitude). Both lists are basically identical, which tells us that receiving the Word into our lives is the same as being filled with the Spirit. Also, keep in mind that the Spirit inspired God's Word. He also illumines it so that we can understand and appropriate it (1 Corinthians 2:12–14; 1 John 2:20,27).

Finally, it is the Spirit who creates and builds up the community of God's people. He empowers us to witness and equips every believer with spiritual gifts that help the body grow (Acts 1:8; 1 Corinthians 12). Sometimes we limit the power of the Spirit or think, 'What difference can I make? I'm just one person.' But God doesn't ask us to witness to everyone — just the person next to us. It's like the story of the little boy walking on the beach.

> Suddenly the boy came upon thousands of starfish that had washed up on the beach. The tide was going out, and for some strange reason, the starfish ended up stuck on the beach. They were all doomed because they couldn't survive being out of the water in the hot sun until the next high tide. The little boy realised this and frantically started picking up starfish and throwing them, one at a time, back into the water.
>
> A man who was walking along the beach saw the boy doing this, and he yelled at the boy, 'Son, what in the world are you doing? Don't you know that there are thousands of starfish on this beach? And don't you know that this beach goes for miles and miles? There is no way in the world you can save all those starfish!'
>
> The little boy thought about that for a moment, then turned to the man and said, 'Yeah, I know. But I can save this one.'
>
> And he heaved it as far as he could into the ocean.[8]

The Yearning to Be Filled

Augustine, in his writings, tells us that in his early years his attitude was, 'Lord, save me from my sins — but not yet.' If we want to be filled with the Spirit, we must have a genuine desire to live a holy life. Speaking of the promised Holy Spirit and the transformation of life that He would bring, Jesus said, '"If anyone is thirsty, let him come to me and drink. Whoever believes in me, as the Scripture has said, streams of living water will flow from within him." By this he meant the Spirit, whom those who believed in him were later to receive' (John 7:37–39). The requirement for experiencing the flow of living water within us is thirst, which is one of the strongest natural yearnings that humans have. If we want to experience the Spirit's filling, we must have a genuine thirst for holiness. A. W. Tozer rightly said, 'Every man is as holy as he really wants to be. But the want must be all-compelling.... Every man is as full of the Spirit as he wants to be....'[9]

Jesus said, 'When he, the Spirit of truth, comes, he will guide you into all truth' (John 16:13). This may be the Holy Spirit's greatest work on our behalf because Jesus said, 'You will know the truth, and *the truth will set you free*' (John 8:32, emphasis added). The truth is not an enemy seeking to expose us, it is a liberating friend!

Jesus also said, 'Men loved darkness instead of light because their deeds were evil' (John 3:19). The Lord loves us too much to allow us to hide, cover up, and walk in darkness. We may fear exposure, but that fear is not from God. Demons fear exposure. They are like cockroaches; they come out at night and run for the shadows when you turn on the light. In contrast, 'God is light; in him there is no darkness at all' (1 John 1:5). The Holy Spirit will guide us out of darkness and into the light, where we can enjoy fellowship with God and other believers. The Holy Spirit is first and foremost the Spirit of truth, and He leads us into all truth. Our responsibility is to respond to that truth by faith.

Coming Up Higher

Read

Galatians 5:16; Ephesians 5:18; 4:30; 1 Thessalonians 5:19.

Reflect

Every part of our Christian life is performed by the power of the Holy Spirit. Can you think of any area in your life you are trying to manage apart from the power of the Spirit?

What would walking by the Spirit or walking more by the Spirit look like in your life?

What hinders your fellowship with the Spirit? What can you do to improve your relationship with the Spirit?

Walking by the Spirit requires that we be sensitive to sin. How are you vulnerable to wrong actions, selfish desires, or fleshly thoughts? How have you turned from or renounced these sins?

How is your prayer life right now? How is your time in the Word helping you sense the Spirit's leading?

What can you do to develop a greater thirst for the Spirit?

Respond

Father God, teach me to live by Your Spirit. Holy Spirit, empower me to live a life that bears fruit for the kingdom and gives glory to the Father. I ask You now, Lord God, to show me where I am hindering the Spirit's work in my life. Show me my sin. And show me, too, what I can do in my prayer life, my Bible-study times, and my fellowship to receive more of the Spirit. Most of all, Lord, make me thirsty for Your Spirit that I may know His power to help me be who You created me to be and what I am in Christ. In His name I pray, amen.

Loneliness is the first thing which
God's eye named not good.

— *John Milton*

Growing in Holiness

We are a generation that loves to be left alone, a generation of loners. But God has called us to come together and be part of His church, the body of Christ. The body needs you, and you need the body. Yet some young people put more time, thought, and effort into what kind of tennis player they are, than they do picking a good church youth group. God conveys Himself and His truth to us through other believers. The British poet John Donne expressed an important truth about human nature when he said, 'No man is an island, entire of itself; every man is a piece of the continent, a part of the main.'

According to the Bible, we are not designed to grow in isolation from other believers. God's intention is for us to grow together as part of a community. God's declaration, 'It is not good for the man to be alone' is related to Christian growth as much as any other part of human life (see Genesis 2:18). Sanctification is not just a matter of *I* or *me*. The New Testament commonly speaks of holiness using the terms *we* and *our*. In the NASB, the word *saints* is used sixty times, but *saint* only appears once. Christian community is God's idea, and a loving unity in the family of God is a big part of growing in sanctification. It is also the means of sanctification. In our culture, we have been trained to be self-centred rather than corporate body-centred as this true story illustrates.

> Not long after the IQ (Intelligence Quotient) test was developed several studies were conducted to find out how different groups of people scored on the test. The test was administered to men and women, young and old, rich and poor, of various cultural backgrounds. It was in this context that the IQ test was given to a group of Hopi Indians.
>
> When the Hopi received the test, they immediately started to ask each other questions and to compare their answers. The instructor saw this happening and quickly intervened, telling them that they each had to take the test alone. 'You are not permitted to help each other or to share your answers among yourselves,' he told them.
>
> When the Hopi heard this, they were outraged and refused to take the test, saying, 'It is not important that I am smarter than my brother, or that my brother is smarter than me. It is only important what we can do together!'[1]

The Need for Fellowship

From time to time, God may allow special circumstances in which a believer is forced into isolation from fellow Christians, as has been the experience of those who have encountered persecution or imprisonment as a result of their professions of faith. In such cases, God conveys His grace directly and sufficiently. But normally He gives Himself to us corporately through His presence in the lives of others. The Bible reveals that our relationships with one another and with God are closely interwoven and sometimes difficult to separate. Our fellowship is both with God and with other believers (1 John 1:3). John also said that 'if we love one another, God lives in us and his love is made complete in us' (1 John 4:12).

Sanctification requires that we pay attention to the command in Hebrews 10:24,25: 'Let us consider how we may spur one another on towards love and good deeds. Let us not give up meeting together, as some are in the habit of doing, but let us encourage one another.' The relationship between fellowship and growth towards holiness becomes more obvious when we consider our real nature as human beings and how our personal growth is intertwined with that of others.

Fellowship Restores Our True Nature

In sanctification we not only share in the holiness of God, but also our true nature is being restored. The true nature of our humanity is realised only in community. The Bible gives us evidence that a person is destined to be fully human only in relationship to other people. It is clear from God's statement that it is not good for people to be alone, that we as humans were not designed to live in isolation from our fellow human beings. (By the way, the root of the Hebrew word for *alone* means 'to separate, to isolate'.)

─────────── Check It Out! ───────────

We were created 'in the image of God' — in the image of a
fellowship of three Persons; we were not created to live alone.

God's remedy for the first Adam's aloneness was to create another human being. While it's true that this remedy focuses on the marriage relationship between man and woman, it also affirms a truth about human beings. We were designed to live in relationships. To be human is to be co-human. Our community nature is also evident from the fact that we were created 'in the image of God' (see Genesis 1:26,27). God is triune: the Father, the Son, and the Holy Spirit — three Persons in one personal being. Although we cannot fully understand the Trinity, we can know with certainty that God is a social being. Involved in His one being is a fellowship of three Persons. And these Persons are what they are only in relationship to each other. For example, the Father would not be the Father except for His relationship to the Son and the Spirit. Likewise, the Son would not be the Son without being related to the Father and also the Spirit.

We were created 'in the image of God' — in the image of a fellowship of three Persons; we were not created to live alone. We were created to live in community, in fellowship with others. It is interesting that the very name *man* (Hebrew, *Adam*) is the name of both the first human and humanity as a whole. Man is both personal and corporate. If we are to grow as Christians, we cannot grow in isolation from other people. If we fail to live in fellowship together we will never understand all that God has for us. We won't be able to see the whole — only experience a part.

> In an ancient village all the people were blind. One day, while walking on the road, six men from that village came upon a man riding an elephant. The six men who had heard about elephants but had never been close to one asked the rider to allow them to touch the great beast. They wanted to go back to their village to tell the other villagers what an elephant looked like.
>
> In great anticipation they returned to their village to report their experience. The villagers gathered around to hear about the elephant.
>
> The first man, who had felt the animal's side said, 'An elephant is like a great thick wall.'

'Nonsense,' said the second man, who had felt the elephant's tusk. 'He is rather short, round, and smooth, but very sharp. I would compare an elephant not with a wall but with a spear.'

The third man, who had touched an ear, took exception. 'It is nothing at all like a wall or a spear,' he said. 'It is like a gigantic leaf made of thick wool carpet. It moves when you touch it.'

'I disagree,' said the fourth man, who had handled the trunk. 'I can tell you that an elephant is like a giant snake.'

The fifth man shouted his disapproval. He had touched one of the elephant's legs and concluded, 'An elephant is round and thick, like a tree.'

The sixth man had been allowed to ride on the elephant's back, and he protested, 'Can none of you accurately describe an elephant? Clearly he is like a gigantic moving mountain!'

To this day, the men continue to argue, and no one in the village has any idea what an elephant looks like.[2]

To find out what God is like we need the body — *everyone* sharing the truth that God has taught him or her. If we stay isolated and alone we'll miss the true nature of God — just like the blind men missed the truth about the elephant.

Fellowship Affirms Our Identity

Another aspect of faith that points to the fact we were designed to live in fellowship is the realisation that our personal identity comes from our relationships. In Western culture, where we emphasise individuality, we often think that individuality and sharing in a group are opposites — that our individuality is lost when we become part of a group. But the opposite is true. We gain our true selfhood by sharing in community.

Have you ever noticed that the uniqueness of our individual

identities emerges as we build relationships with others? For example, the individuality of a man and a woman becomes more apparent after they are joined in marriage. This is also apparent in the Bible's often-used metaphor of the church as a body. If we were to find a body part that was separated from the rest of the body, and we have no knowledge of its relation to the body, we would not be able to identify what it really was — its nature, purpose, and function. A toe or kneecap by itself would appear to serve no useful purpose. We would simply identify it as a useless blob of flesh or bone. It acquires its identity only in relation to the other parts of the body.

So our personal individualities — who we really are — come only in relation to God, our families, fellow believers, and others. Our human nature and divine purpose are not fully realised except in community.

It's important to note that sin disrupts the corporate body. When we choose to live independently of God, we not only alienate ourselves from the Creator but also from other humans. Sin brings an isolation that is the ruin of human community.

Our Oneness in Christ

If we require community to know fulfilment as humans, then Christian growth also requires community for us to reach our God-designed potential. Christian growth seeks the progressive conquering of the sin that alienates us. This allows God's intention of human community to be more fully realised. That is why Jesus prayed in the 'high priestly prayer' that we all be one as He and the Father are one:

> My prayer is not for them alone. I pray also for those who will believe in me through their message, that all of them may be one, Father, just as you are in me and I am in you. May they also be in us so that the world may believe that you have sent me. I have given them the glory that you gave me, that they may be one as we are one: I in them

and you in me. May they be brought to complete unity to let the world know that you sent me and have loved them even as you have loved me (John 17:20–23).

The book of Ephesians talks about this as well. It is God's goal to 'bring all things in heaven and on earth together under one head, even Christ' (1:10). We as believers in Christ are the first phase of this overall purpose. Likewise, the most alienated people in New Testament times, the Jews and the Gentiles, were in Christ made into 'one new man' (2:15).

Since the fall, every attempt to unite humanity on any basis other than Jesus Christ has ended in failure. God will continue to thwart the plans of man even as He did at the tower of Babel. People may try to become united for a common cause, but such efforts will last only for a season. As soon as the crisis that calls them together is resolved, they will fall apart and most likely realign themselves to their ethnic identities, religious preferences, or class distinctions. For example, Communism held Yugoslavia together by sheer force under the rule of Marshal Tito, but as soon as the external yoke was thrown off, the country splintered into Slovenia, Croatia, Bosnia, and Serbia. Even the body of Christ becomes divided when we seek our identity in something other than Christ.

To put all this in terms of sanctification, our being set apart unto God not only clothes us with Christ, but it also makes us a new, unified humanity. When we personally come to Christ, we find ourselves one with all others in Him. Galatians 3:28 says, 'You are all one in Christ Jesus.' This oneness is not only with Christ, it is with one another: 'We are members of one another' (Ephesians 4:25 NASB); 'we, who are many, are one body in Christ, and individually members one of another' (Romans 12:5 NASB).

Being part of the body of Christ is extremely important and vital to our Christian health. How can we share this gift with others? What does the following story tell us?

There was once an old monastery that had fallen upon hard times. Centuries earlier, it had been a thriving monastery where many dedicated monks lived and worked and had great influence on the realm. But now only five monks lived there, and they were all over seventy years old. This was clearly a dying order.

A few miles from the monastery lived an old hermit who many thought was a prophet. One day as the monks agonised over the impending demise of their order, they decided to visit the hermit to see if he might have some advice for them. Perhaps he would be able to see the future and show them what they could do to save the monastery.

The hermit welcomed the five monks to his hut, but when they explained the purpose of their visit, the hermit could only commiserate with them. 'Yes, I understand how it is,' said the hermit. 'The spirit has gone out of the people. Hardly anyone cares much for the old things any more.'

'Is there anything you can tell us,' the abbot [head monk] enquired of the hermit, 'that would help us save the monastery?'

'No, I'm sorry,' said the hermit. 'I don't know how your monastery can be saved. The only thing that I can tell you is that one of you is an apostle of God.'

The monks were both disappointed and confused by the hermit's cryptic statement. They returned to the monastery, wondering what the hermit could have meant by the statement, 'One of you is an apostle of God.' For months after their visit, the monks pondered the significance of the hermit's words.

'One of us is an apostle of God,' they mused. 'Did he actually mean one of us monks here at the monastery? That's impossible. We are all too old. We are too insignificant. On the other hand, what if it's true? And if it is true, then which one of us is it? Do you suppose he meant the abbot? Yes, if he meant anyone, he probably meant the abbot. He has been our leader for more than a generation. On the other hand, he might have meant Brother Thomas. Certainly Brother Thomas is a holy man — a man of wisdom and light. He couldn't have meant Brother Elred. Elred gets crotchety at times and is difficult to reason with. On the other hand, he is almost always right. Maybe the hermit did mean Brother Elred. But surely he could not have meant Brother Phillip. Phillip is so passive, so shy — a real nobody. Still, he's always there when you need him. He's loyal and trustworthy. Yes, suppose he did? Suppose I am an apostle of God? Oh, God, not me. I couldn't be that much for you. Or could I?'

As they contemplated in this manner, the old monks began to treat each other with extraordinary respect on the off chance that one of them might actually be an apostle of God. And on the off chance that each monk himself might be the apostle spoken of by the hermit, each monk began to treat himself with extraordinary respect.

Because the monastery was situated in a beautiful forest, many people came there to picnic on its tiny lawn and to walk on its paths, and now and then they would even go into the tiny chapel to meditate. As they did so, without even being conscious of it, they sensed the aura of extraordinary respect that now began to surround the five old monks and seemed to radiate out of them, permeating the atmosphere of the place. There was something strangely attractive, even compelling about it. Hardly knowing why, people began to come to bring their friends to show them this special place. And their friends brought their friends.

As more and more visitors came, some of the younger men started to talk with the old monks. After a while, one asked if he could join them. Then another. And another. Within a few years the monastery had once again become a thriving order and, thanks to the hermit's gift, a vibrant centre of light and spirituality throughout the realm.[3]

Sometimes, just like the old monks, we ask, 'How can we attract more people to our youth group? How can we get some new life in here and grow, both in numbers and spiritually?' Perhaps the answer has to do with how we regard and treat each other and ourselves. Are we always putting each other down and creating an atmosphere of criticism and negativism? Or are we treating each other with extraordinary dignity and respect?

Why don't you take a moment and read John 17 — it's not very long. It records Jesus' prayer to His Father for the church, for you and me. What did He pray for? He asked that all of us would be one so the world might believe. When we care for each other and treat each other with love and respect, then those in the world find the church to be attractive, even compelling. Let's stop fighting and hurting each other and be one body in Christ. This oneness is expressed over and over again in the book of Ephesians:

- We are all 'fellow citizens' (2:19).
- We are joined *together* to become a holy temple and built *together* to become a dwelling in which God lives by his Spirit (see 2:21,22).
- The gospel has made us all 'heirs together', 'members together', and 'sharers together' (3:6).

Living Out Our Unity

As soon as we are set apart, we are joined together in Christ by the Spirit. You'll recall that in chapter 5 we discovered that our progressive sanctification is aimed at making real the truths of our positional sanctification. So at the beginning of his instructions about how we are to live, Paul tells us to live out the unity that is a reality in the body. He says:

Be completely humble and gentle; be patient, bearing with one another in love. Make every effort to keep the unity of the Spirit through the bond of peace. There is one body and one Spirit — just as you were called to one hope when you were called — one Lord, one faith, one baptism; one God and Father of all, who is over all and through all and in all (Ephesians 4:2–6).

Relationships and Growth

In the Bible it is easy to see that spiritual growth means growth in our ability to live in harmony with others. In one way or another, almost all the 'deeds of the flesh' — sexual immorality, impurity, debauchery (sensuality), idolatry, witchcraft, hatred, discord, jealousy, rage, selfish ambition, drunkenness — cause relationships to break up. The 'fruit of the Spirit' — love, joy, peace, patience, kindness, goodness, faithfulness, gentleness, self-control — encourages relationships (see Galatians 5:19–23). Growth in our spiritual life means growth in relationships. This social growth is not simply the goal of individual growth; a person can't grow in isolation and then get along with others better.

The truth that sanctification or spiritual growth takes place as a result of relationships between believers is a strong theme in Scripture. One of the key concepts used to speak of spiritual progress is called 'building up' or 'edification'. Except for one debated verse, all of the key expressions used to speak of genuine edification are oriented towards other people. We are encouraged to build up our neighbour (Romans 15:2) and to edify 'the other' (1 Corinthians 14:17). 'Mutual edification,' or the building up of 'each other,' is also commanded in Romans 14:19 and 1 Thessalonians 5:11.

Most often the concept of edification or building up is used in relation to the functioning of Christian community. Spiritual gifts that strengthen the church are to be commended (1 Corinthians 14:4,12). The metaphors of the church as a building and a body clearly teach growth in relationships.

When Paul said that we 'are being built together to become a dwelling in which God lives by his Spirit' (Ephesians 2:22), he was not talking about people who are growing individually, but a group of believers who are unified through relationships. Peter described us as 'living stones' all united to 'the living Stone' and being built into one 'spiritual house' (1 Peter 2:4,5).

The dynamic of sanctification in relation to other people is clearly evident in the Bible's picture of the church as a body. We know that in our own physical bodies, the various parts grow only as they are in union with the rest of the body. Likewise, union with the body of Christ — other believers — is indispensable to the growth of every individual believer.

Relationships and Knowledge

Finally, the knowledge of spiritual matters is not gained alone. Rather, it is gained through interaction with other believers. Paul prayed that we as believers 'may have power, *together with all the saints*, to grasp how wide and long and high and deep is the love of Christ, and to know this love that surpasses knowledge — that you may be filled to the measure of all the fullness of God' (Ephesians 3:18,19, emphasis added). In Ephesians 4:12–16, Paul once again talks about how maturity in faith and knowledge takes place when those in the body of Christ are involved in building up one another:

> … to prepare God's people for works of service, so that the body of Christ may be built up until we all reach unity in the faith and in the knowledge of the Son of God and become mature, attaining to the whole measure of the fullness of Christ. Then we will no longer be infants, tossed back and forth by the waves, and blown here and there by every wind of teaching and by the cunning and craftiness of men in their deceitful scheming. Instead, speaking the truth in love, we will in all things grow up into him who is the Head, that is, Christ. From him the

whole body, joined and held together by every support-
ing ligament, grows and builds itself up in love, as each
part does its work.

As each of us contributes our part to the rest of the body, we
come to a better understanding of the spiritual matters that
help to nourish our life and growth.

Spiritual growth, then, is more than personal; it is communal. God conveys Himself to each of us not only through our
personal relations with Him and our practice of the spiritual disciplines, but also through other believers as we fellowship with
them.

The Benefits of Fellowship

Fellowship Provides Strength

There is a strengthening of faith when it is shared in common
with others. It is too difficult for us to stand alone and be bom-
barded with the lies of the world. Sharing the same beliefs and
values with one another in close fellowship provides the
strength that we need individually.

How strong is mutual faith? An interesting picture is provided for us in the 'shield of faith,' part of each believer's
armour against the attacks of the enemy (see Ephesians 6:16).
The Roman soldiers in the New Testament era used a huge,
door-shaped body shield that provided a lot of personal protection. But even more protection was offered when the soldiers
came together as a compact unit and held these large shields
side-by-side in front or raised above them (against arrows and
spears). If they stood apart and held their shields individually,
their sides were exposed, but when they brought their shields
together, they were fully protected.

Fellowship Provides Learning

Learning is another aspect of spiritual growth that best takes
place in the context of Christian fellowship. We can gain help-

ful insights from the teaching of gifted individuals whom God has given to the church. We can also benefit from the sharing of truth by all believers. No one person has all the spiritual gifts, nor can any one person thoroughly perceive God's truth on his or her own. We can learn and grow from one another's experiences and perspectives. Learning can also take place through observation; to see the truth modelled in another life can be more powerful than simply knowing it intellectually.

Fellowship Provides Accountability

The writer to the Hebrews tells us to encourage one another daily (Hebrews 3:13). Fellowship, accountability, and love can make all the difference in a person's life. For instance, let's look at this account of Howard Hendricks' life.

> By the fifth grade, I was bearing all the fruit of a kid who feels insecure, unloved and pretty angry at life. In other words, I was tearing the place apart. However, my teacher Miss Simon apparently thought that I was blind to the problem because she regularly reminded me, 'Howard, you are the worst behaved child in this school!'
>
> *So tell me something I don't already know!* I thought to myself, as I proceeded to live up (or down) to her opinion of me....
>
> Needless to say, the fifth grade was probably the worst year of my life. Finally I was graduated — for obvious reasons. But I left with Miss Simon's words ringing in my ears: 'Howard, you are the worst behaved child in this school!'
>
> You can imagine what my expectations were upon entering the sixth grade. The first day of class, my teacher, Miss Noe, went down the roll call, and it wasn't long before she came to my name. 'Howard Hendricks,' she called out, glancing from her list to where I was sitting with my arms folded, just waiting to go into action. She looked me over for a moment and then she said, 'I've

heard a lot about you.' Then she smiled and added, 'But I don't believe a word of it.'

I tell you, that moment was a fundamental turning point not only in my education, but in my life. Suddenly, unexpectedly, someone believed in me. For the first time in my life, someone saw potential in me. Miss Noe put me on special assignments. She gave me little jobs to do. She invited me to come in after school to work on my reading and arithmetic. She challenged me with a higher standard.

I had a hard time letting her down. In fact, one time I got so involved in one of her homework assignments that I stayed up until 1:30 in the morning working on it! Eventually my father came down the hall and said, 'What's the matter, son? Are you sick?'

'No, I'm doing my homework,' I replied.

He kind of blinked and rubbed his eyes, not quite sure whether he was awake. He'd never heard me say anything like that before.

What made the difference between fifth and sixth? The fact that someone was willing to give me a chance. Someone was willing to believe in me while challenging me with higher expectations. That was risky because there was no guarantee that I would honour Miss Noe's trust.

Everyone likes the end product of mentoring, especially when it yields a peak performer — the star athlete, the successful business person, the brilliant lawyer, the impressive communicator. But how many of us want to deal with the person at the front end of the process?[4]

We are all called to those around us who need encouragement, and we all certainly need it!

The Pre-eminence of Relationships

The order in which Paul presented the information in his epistles reveals another important truth about our sanctification in the context of relationships: God works in our lives primarily through committed relationships. In the book of Colossians, Paul first presents the finished work of Christ, then he talks about establishing God's people in Christ, and finally he discusses moving Christians towards maturity. We learn in the first two chapters that we are transferred into the kingdom of Christ, forgiven, established in Him, and that the devil has been defeated. Chapter 3 begins with the challenge to set our eyes on things above and to put off the 'old man' (our pre-Christian nature) and put on the new man, 'which is being renewed in knowledge in the image of its Creator. Here there is no Greek or Jew, circumcised or uncircumcised, barbarian, Scythian, slave or free, but Christ is all, and is in all' (Colossians 3:10,11). In other words, there should be no racial, religious, social, or cultural barriers in the body of Christ. We are unified in Him.

After establishing our identity in Christ, Paul gives us guidelines for developing character. Notice that his instructions are all relationship-oriented:

> As God's chosen people, holy and dearly loved, clothe yourselves with compassion, kindness, humility, gentleness and patience. Bear with each other and forgive whatever grievances you may have against one another. Forgive as the Lord forgave you. And over all these virtues put on love, which binds them all together in perfect unity (Colossians 3:12–14).

The Keys to Great Fellowship

Someone once said that living in the context of committed relationships is like living in Noah's ark: 'We wouldn't be able to stand the stink inside if it weren't for the storm outside!'

There may be some truth in that, but living together would be a lot easier if we would all fulfil two key responsibilities:

1. Conform to the image of God.

We cannot blame other people for hindering us from becoming the people God created us to be. We must assume our own responsibility for our characters. According to Paul, that is essentially God's will for our lives: 'It is God's will that you should be sanctified' (1 Thessalonians 4:3). And the sanctification process can be difficult. From Proverbs we know that 'as iron sharpens iron, so one man sharpens another' (27:17). There is always going to be friction when iron sharpens iron, but the sparks that fly are a sign that the rough edges are being smoothed out.

2. Love one another.

We do this by accepting one another as Christ accepted us and by laying down our lives for one another as Christ laid down His life for us (see Romans 15:7; 1 John 3:16).

Imagine what would happen in our homes and churches if everybody assumed responsibility for their own growth in character and everybody made a commitment to meet one another's needs. Our homes and churches would be more like heaven than Noah's ark, and we would all be more like Jesus!

Coming Up Higher

Read

Galatians 3:28; Ephesians 4:2–6, 16, 25; Romans 12:5.

Reflect

Why would fellowship with other believers be so important to your sanctification?

When has God used a relationship with a brother or sister in the Lord (fellowship) as a means of sanctification for you?

What rough edges have been smoothed by God through fellowship with His people so that you could be more solidly joined together with other believers?

Read Ephesians 4:16. Remember how the Roman soldiers held their door-shaped shield together to protect each other? How do we as the body of Christ protect and stand together?

Think about adding one committed relationship with a strong believer to your week. What sacrifices would need to be made? How would you benefit from this relationship?

Respond

Almighty God, I thank You that even though I can't be discipled directly by the physical presence of Jesus, I can be discipled by His people. Thank You for conveying Yourself — Your love and grace, Your hope and truth — to us through other believers. And I thank You that fellowship with other believers restores our true nature and affirms our identity as believers. Help me to be willing to take responsibility for my own character. Also help me and my friends to be willing to love one another so that we may contribute to the Christian community. In Jesus' name I pray, amen.

> When we came to Jesus Christ, we repented. We 'crucified' everything we knew to be wrong. We took our old self-centred nature, with all its sinful passions and desires, and nailed it to the cross. And this repentance of ours was decisive, as decisive as a crucifixion.[1]
>
> — *John Stott*

8

The Struggle

We begin our Christian walk looking like a lump of coal. But every child of God is a diamond in the rough. Given enough time and pressure, every lump of coal eventually becomes a brilliant diamond. It's interesting to note that if you remove coal from the pressures of the earth and introduce impurities into its chemical composition, it will never become a diamond. Staying pure and remaining under pressure is what forms the diamond. The same is true for us as Christians. Unlike coal, however, we have a part to play in the process of growing up.

The fact that sanctification is a supernatural work could lead us to believe that we should simply let God do all the work; we should 'let go and let God.' Like a lump of coal, we could relinquish any effort or responsibility on our part and let God control us while we rest in His power. We tend to think this way because, ultimately, sanctification is God's work. Victory over sin is possible only through the finished work of Christ. Progressive sanctification takes place when we abide in Christ and live by the power of the Holy Spirit. God is the one who causes growth (1 Corinthians 3:6), and there is a certain rest for the believer in the finished work of Christ. For instance, we don't need to strive for God's acceptance. In light of all that, however, Scripture presents the process of Christian growth as far more than just sitting around.

A Radical Pursuit

Paul tells us to 'work out [our] salvation with fear and trembling' even as God 'works in [us] to will and to act according to his good purpose' (Philippians 2:12,13). God prepared good works for us to do, but we are to do them. Working out our salvation is a tough process that involves sacrifice and suffering. It is more like an athletic event than a tea party. Paul said the Christian life is like a race that we should run to win: 'Forgetting what is behind and straining towards what is ahead, I press on towards the goal to win the prize for which God has called me heavenwards in Christ Jesus' (Philippians 3:13,14). The Greek word for *press* is the same one used elsewhere for *persecute*, and suggests a determined pursuit. A determined, radical pursuit is talked about in 1 Corinthians 9:24–27; Paul spoke like a coach rallying his team to victory in the game of life:

> Do you not know that in a race all the runners run, but only one gets the prize? Run in such a way as to get the prize. Everyone who competes in the games goes into strict training. They do it to get a crown that will not last; but we do it to get a crown that will last forever. Therefore I do not run like a man running aimlessly; I do not fight like a man beating the air. No, I beat my body and make

it my slave so that after I have preached to others, I myself will not be disqualified for the prize.

Every major league baseball player has to attend spring training. Even the veterans are drilled again and again in the basics of their sport. What if Mark McGuire said, 'I'm a pro and I hit a lot of home runs. I don't need to practise my hitting.' First, he would be a detriment to a good team working together, and no good coach puts up with that attitude. But 'Big Mac' does practise, and he'll go down as one of the greatest home-run hitters in history because he hit seventy homers in a single season. If people are willing to have that kind of commitment to the game of baseball, can we do no less in the game of life played for the glory of God?

Paul said, 'Train yourself to be godly' (1 Timothy 4:7). We get the English word *gymnasium* from the Greek word for *train*, which suggests rigorous exercise in things related to godliness. Sanctification requires us to ground ourselves in the basics of our faith and then discipline ourselves to live according to what God says is true.

An Ongoing Battle

Whether we like it or not, we are in a battle against evil forces — a battle that is described as a 'struggle' or, more literally, a 'wrestling'. The Greek word describes a 'hand-to-hand fight.'[2] Paul wrote to Timothy, 'I give you this instruction in keeping with the prophecies once made about you, so that by following them you may fight the good fight' (1 Timothy 1:18). Later he added, 'You, man of God, flee from all this [temptation and harmful desires], and pursue righteousness, godliness, faith, love, endurance and gentleness. Fight the good fight of the faith' (1 Timothy 6:11,12). In his second epistle to Timothy, he said, 'Endure hardship with us like a good soldier' (2 Timothy 2:3). Then at the end of his ministry, Paul said, 'I have fought the good fight, I have finished the race' (2 Timothy 4:7).

Paul's instructions reveal that the Christian life is not an effortless lifestyle. We are to enter into a lifestyle that struggles against sin in all its forms. At the cross, Christ won the battle over the powers of sin, but in God's plan, the defeated enemies have not yet been judged. They still wage war against God. And, in a real sense, the battleground for the ongoing war between Christ and sin is now in our lives. Our coming to Christ means enlistment in His army to do battle against sin.

We are able to enter the fray armed with Christ's victory because we wage war 'in Christ'. Our ultimate victory is certain, but that does not eliminate the present battle. In fact, the closer we grow to Christ, the more the battle is likely to intensify.

We struggle against sin because it opposes us in our active process of growing spiritually. But we also struggle with the impersonal effects of sin — effects such as the suffering of physical sicknesses and diseases, grief and death, and emotional turmoil. That's what Paul was talking about in 2 Corinthians 6:3–10:

> We put no stumbling block in anyone's path, so that our ministry will not be discredited. Rather, as servants of God we commend ourselves in every way: in great endurance; in troubles, hardships and distresses; in beatings, imprisonments and riots; in hard work, sleepless nights and hunger; in purity, understanding, patience and kindness; in the Holy Spirit and in sincere love; in truthful speech and in the power of God; with weapons of righteousness in the right hand and in the left; through glory and dishonour, bad report and good report; genuine, yet regarded as impostors; known, yet regarded as unknown; dying, and yet we live on; beaten, and yet not killed; sorrowful, yet always rejoicing; poor, yet making many rich; having nothing, and yet possessing everything.

The Traitor Within

Scripture reveals that one of the opponents of our Christian growth is very close at hand. In fact, it is within us! Our *flesh* has sinful desires that oppose God. Paul wrote, 'For I know nothing good dwells in me, that is, in my flesh; for the wishing is present in me, but the doing of the good is not.... With my flesh [I serve] the law of sin' (Romans 7:18,25 NASB). The desires of the flesh are opposed to the desires of the Spirit of God within us (Galatians 5:16,17). They are also opposed to us and our sanctification. Peter said that we are to 'abstain from fleshly lusts, which wage war against the soul' (1 Peter 2:11 NASB).

Defining the Flesh

The term *flesh* has many meanings in the Bible. It can refer to the physical body. Paul refers to the physical body when he spoke of a bodily illness (see Galatians 4:13; 2:20). Flesh can also refer to the human person, as the parallel in the following verse shows: 'This is what the Lord says: "Cursed is the one who trusts in man, who depends on flesh for his strength"' (Jeremiah 17:5). The prophet Isaiah declared that 'all flesh' will see the glory of the Lord, but then went on to say that all flesh is grass and the grass withers (see Isaiah 40:5–7). Another physical reference is found in John 1:14 referring to the Son of God's willingness to take on humanity: 'the Word [became] flesh.'

—————————— Check It Out! ——————————

The flesh seeks life on human terms and standards rather than God's.

In those uses of the word *flesh*, there is no concept of sinfulness or evil. The common element is weakness. Compared to the spirit, which has life and power, the physical flesh is weak. This is clear in God's chiding of His people for seeking help from the Egyptian armies instead of Himself: 'The Egyptians are men and not God; their horses are flesh and not spirit' (Isaiah 31:3). The weakness of the flesh is seen also in the psalmist's fearlessness of man: 'In God I have put my trust; I shall not be afraid. What can mere man [literally, *flesh*] do to me?' (Psalm 56:4 NASB). A good illustration of this principle is our day-to-day attitude about food. In the 'fight' between healthy eating and consuming junk food — which one usually wins? Here's the incredible 'loser diet' we all experience:

Breakfast
1/2 grapefruit
1 slice whole wheat toast
8 oz. skim milk

Lunch
4 oz. chicken
1 cup steamed courgette
1 biscuit
Milk

Mid-Afternoon Snack
Rest of the package of biscuits
1 quart chocolate ice cream
1 jar hot fudge

Dinner
2 loaves garlic bread
Large pepperoni-and-mushroom pizza
Large bottle of Coke
2 Snickers bars
5 ice creams
Entire cheesecake, eaten directly from the fridge

Diet Tips:
- If no one sees you eat it, it has no calories.
- If you drink a diet soda with a candy bar, they cancel each other out.
- When eating with someone else, calories don't count.

- Food used for medical purposes never counts (includes hot chocolate, toast, and cheesecake).
- If you fatten up everyone else around you, then you look thinner.
- Movie-related foods don't count because they are part of the entire entertainment experience and not part of one's personal fuel.
- Biscuit pieces contain no calories. The process of breakage causes calorie leakage.[3]

That diet sounds like the flesh is running the show, doesn't it?

Living in the Flesh

The use of *flesh* when referring to man's desire to sin is often used in the New Testament, especially in the writings of Paul. This flesh may be defined very simply: existence apart from God. The fleshly life is dominated by sin and a drive that opposes God. A person who walks by the flesh is self-centred rather than God-centred. In short, the flesh seeks life on human terms and standards rather than God's. It is the human tendency to rely on self rather than God.

It is this idea of weakness that develops into the use of the term *flesh* for that which is sinful to God. Man, as flesh, is a morally frail creature. Apart from God, man is no match for the power of sin; consequently, humanity comes under its bondage.

The apostle spoke of people who put confidence in the flesh. They boast 'in the flesh' because man tends to glory in his own accomplishments. According to the Bible, people 'outside of Christ' live in the flesh. Alienated from God, they live in bondage to sinful, self-centred existences as their own gods. They not only live in the flesh, but they also walk according to the flesh, meaning that their actions and attitudes all bear the characteristics of the flesh. Those who 'live according to the sinful nature [flesh] have their minds set on what that nature desires…. It does not submit to God's law, nor can it do so.

Those controlled by the sinful nature cannot please God' (Romans 8:5,7,8).

But Paul eventually came to realise that the only proper ground for boasting was in 'the cross of our Lord Jesus Christ' (Galatians 6:14). Salvation in Christ brings a radical change in our relation to the flesh, but it doesn't eliminate it as a foe. In fact, we will experience more intense struggles with our flesh as the enemy of God now that we are Christians.

Breaking the Power of the Flesh

For believers who are 'in Christ', sin's dominion through the flesh has been broken. We 'are not in the flesh but in the Spirit' (Romans 8:9 NASB). In our death with Christ we have made a radical break with the flesh. Paul said that 'those who belong to Christ Jesus have crucified the flesh with its passions and desires' (Galatians 5:24 NASB). This brings us to a question that many Christians struggle with: If the flesh has been crucified, why do we still have trouble with it?

It is important to recognise that our crucifixion of the flesh is not the same as the crucifixion of the 'old man' or 'old self' (Romans 6:6; see also Galatians 2:20). The latter took place when, through faith, we were joined to Christ in His death. That actually happened to us — 'our old self was crucified' (Romans 6:6). Each of us, as an old creation belonging to the old humanity, was made a new creature and part of the new humanity by God when we became joined to Christ. In all of this, we died, yet each of us lives in newness of life in Christ (see Galatians 2:20).

In the case of the flesh, however, *we* are said to have crucified it — not God. It is not that we died, but rather that we put the flesh to death. We denied our self-centred existence when we came to Christ. Yet the reality of our actions is experienced only in accord with the faith in which it is done. As Stott says in the opening quote of this chapter, we crucified 'everything we knew to be wrong.' And it might be added that we did it with all the faith we had at the time. But our faith (which includes knowledge), while sincere and genuine, was not mature and complete. As the Bible says, we are born again as babies, alive and designed to grow (see 1 Peter 2:2). We grow as we put to use more and more of Christ's life in us by the power of the Spirit. As we grow, the reality of what we did totally in principle — namely, crucifying the flesh and its old self-centred influence — becomes increasingly more real in our experience. We must learn to ignore the flesh and its call to us or we will obey its command. If we don't grow we tend to become lazy and self-satisfied which gives sin an opening. When we sit down with sin, we are like this 'reasonable' hunter:

> Winter was coming on and a hunter went out into the forest to shoot a bear, out of which he planned to make a warm coat. By and by he saw a big bear coming towards him and raised his gun and took aim. 'Wait!' said the bear. 'Why do you want to shoot me?'
>
> 'Because I am cold,' said the hunter, 'and I need a coat.'
>
> 'But I am hungry,' the bear replied. 'Maybe if we just talk this over a little, we could come to a compromise.'
>
> So the hunter sat down beside the bear and began to talk over the pros and cons.
>
> In the end, however, the hunter was well enveloped by the bear's fur, and the bear had eaten his dinner.[4]

As believers, we no longer live in the flesh or listen to its call. Sin's reign over us through the passions and desires of the flesh has been broken. We have decisively said 'no' to the old god-playing existence of the flesh and 'yes' to Christ and the Spirit. The flesh is no longer the dominant, controlling characteristic of our lives. The 'I' of each of us is new. At its core, it is God-oriented. But all of this is centred in the process of growing. The new 'I' has not yet been perfected in faith to walk continually by the Spirit. The characteristics of the old man are still present, albeit no longer representing our true identity. We live in the situation of the 'already/not yet'. The new creation to which we belong has been inaugurated by the work Christ did at His first coming. But our old nature — the old man — has not yet been judged and removed and the perfection of the new man made complete.

In a very real sense the reality of the 'already/not yet' of God's salvation belongs to us personally in this life as well as to the broader history of salvation. Only with final glorification will the new man be perfected. In the meantime the flesh, with its sinful passions and desires, is present to tempt us to indulge in self-centred attitudes and actions. That's why we are told to 'walk by the Spirit, and [we] will not carry out the desire of the flesh' (Galatians 5:16 NASB).

What the Flesh Does

The flesh is a traitor within us whose self-centred desires and passions are the expressions of sin's tempting power. Since human life is many-faceted, the flesh's temptations to gain life apart from God takes many forms. Whether we live a legalistic life of religiosity and good works or an immoral, lawless, pleasure-seeking life, we are still fleshly. Both these lifestyles hold out false promises of gaining life on the basis of our own values and efforts. The apostle Paul said that before he came to Christ, he attempted to gain life according to the flesh:

> If anyone else thinks he has reasons to put confidence in the flesh, I have more: circumcised on the eighth day, of the people of Israel, of the tribe of Benjamin, a Hebrew of Hebrews; in regard to the law, a Pharisee; as for zeal, persecuting the church; as for legalistic righteousness, faultless (Philippians 3:4–6).

After Paul became a Christian, instead of putting his confidence in the flesh, he glorified in Christ and boasted in the cross (Philippians 3:3; Galatians 6:14).

The flesh within us, in relation to the power of sin, is open to the influence of the world system around us, a system dominated by evil powers and the direct operation of evil spirits (see Ephesians 2:1–3; 6:12). The flesh is the pull within us to any and every form of action that is not from God. We might not be at the extremes of fleshly religiosity or uncontrolled living, but when we see within ourselves any desire to exalt self in any form, we can know with certainty that the flesh is still present within us. Simply stated, the flesh is the constant desire to avoid living life through the cross or gaining the true life through giving up our self-centredness.

Check It Out!

It is only as we live in union with Christ by the power of the Spirit that we can overcome the temptations of the flesh.

The Bible clearly shows that we are vulnerable to the sinful desires of our flesh, the traitor within. That's why the Bible is filled with commands to avoid the attitudes and actions of the flesh both in our personal and church life. Because we are no longer dominated by the flesh, we do not have to give in to its desires. Going back to the hunting story, we don't have to talk things over with the bear [sin], we can just shoot [crucify] it!

Correctly Responding to the Flesh

The believer's response to the flesh must begin with the recognition that the power to resist the self-centred life cannot come from self. It must come from a power beyond ourselves. Even as Christians we cannot break the power of sin through the flesh any more than we could as non-Christians. We are powerless against sin and must depend upon a power greater than ourselves. *Victory is available solely through the power of the Spirit,* through the power of the Overcomer.

Louis Pasteur's co-worker in the demonstration of what used to be called the germ theory was Dr Felix Ruh, a Jewish doctor in Paris. The physician's granddaughter had died of black diphtheria, and Dr Ruh, vowing he would find out what had killed his granddaughter, locked himself in his laboratory for days. He emerged with a fierce determination to prove, with his colleague Louis Pasteur, that the germ theory was more than just a theory.

The medical association had disapproved of Pasteur and had succeeded in getting him exiled, but he did not go far from Paris. He hid in the forest and erected a laboratory in which to continue his forbidden research.

Twenty beautiful horses were led out into the forest to the improvised laboratory. Scientists, doctors, and nurses came to watch the experiment. Ruh opened a steel vault and took out a large pail filled with black diphtheria germs, which he had cultured carefully for months. There were enough germs in that pail to kill everyone in France. The scientist went to each horse and swabbed its nostrils, tongue, throat and eyes with the deadly germs. Every horse except one developed a terrific fever and died. Most of the doctors and scientists wearied of the experiment and did not remain for what they thought would be the death of the remaining horse.

For several more days this final horse lingered, lying pathetically on the ground. While Ruh, Pasteur, and several others were sleeping on cots in the stables, the orderly on duty had been instructed to awaken the scientists should there be any change in the animal's temperature during the night.

About 2.00 am the temperature showed a half-degree decrease, and the orderly awakened Dr Ruh. By morning the thermometer had dropped two more degrees. By night the fever was entirely gone, and the horse was able to stand, eat, and drink.

The scientist drew blood from the veins of this animal

that had developed the black diphtheria but had overcome it. The scientists drove as fast as they could to the municipal hospital in Paris. They forced their way past the superintendent and the guards and went into the ward where three hundred babies lay segregated to die from black diphtheria. With the blood of the horse, they inoculated every one of the babies [over the protests of the other doctors]. All but three lived and recovered completely.

They were saved by the blood of an overcomer.

We, too, have been saved by the blood of an overcomer. Jesus Christ overcame sin and death on the cross, and by His blood we are saved. (See Ephesians 1:7.)[5]

We are told to put to death the fleshly deeds of the body by the Spirit. Only when we walk by the Spirit will we not 'carry out the desire of the flesh.' It is only by living in union with Christ and by the power of the Spirit that we can overcome the temptations of the flesh. Only the victorious life of Christ lived in us by the Spirit is sufficient for the task.

Living by the Spirit requires us to believe that all we have and are is in Christ and in the reality of the supernatural power resident within us. But it also takes obedient action. Two specific actions related to the flesh are given in the Bible.

Resisting the Flesh
The first action we're to take against the flesh is found in Romans 8:13: 'If by the Spirit you put to death the misdeeds of the body, you will live.' The Spirit is the power by which the evil desires of the flesh can be resisted, but *we have to participate with Him*. We are to be actively and continually putting to death practices that we know are sinful. 'Those who live according to the sinful nature [flesh] have their minds set on what that nature desires; but those who live in accordance with the Spirit have their minds set on what the spirit desires. The mind of sin-

ful man is death, but the mind controlled by the Spirit is life and peace' (Romans 8:5,6).

Have you ever noticed that people with addictive behaviours have no peace of mind? In fact, many people drink or take drugs to drown out the bothersome thoughts that plague them. Others simply obey the 'voices' in their heads by indulging the flesh in order to gain some temporary respite. By contrast, crucifying the flesh begins by taking every thought captive to the obedience of Christ (2 Corinthians 10:5).

Seek the Things Above
The other action we are to take against the flesh is given in Colossians 3:5: 'Put to death, therefore, whatever belongs to your earthly nature: sexual immorality, impurity, lust, evil desires and greed, which is idolatry.' The preceding context of this verse tells us how we are to do that:

> If then you have been raised up with Christ, keep seeking the things above, where Christ is, seated at the right hand of God. Set your mind on the things above, not on the things that are on earth. For you have died and your life is hidden with Christ in God (Colossians 3:1–3 NASB).

If we mentally focus on earthly things, we will likely carry out the desires of the flesh.

Replacing Fleshly Thoughts with Truth

Fixing our eyes on Jesus, 'the author and perfecter of our faith' (Hebrews 12:2) and learning to discipline our minds to choose the truth greatly determines our progress in sanctification. Only when we know the truth and the character of Christ do we see the ugliness of the flesh. The sanctified heart will always choose freedom over bondage. Only then can we ruthlessly root out and put an end to all the displays of self-centredness.

Look at it this way: How do you get an old bone away from

a hungry dog? You don't want to grab the bone because the dog will fight for it. He will become even more protective of that bone. Throw him a steak, and he will spit out the bone. Chances are that the dog will bury the old bone so he will have something to return to if life becomes a little lean. And he may be tempted to dig it up again to make sure it's still available in case he gets hungry again. As Christians, we need to bury the deeds of the flesh and take a good look at Jesus when we are tempted to dig them up. Nothing else will satisfy like Jesus. 'Blessed are those who hunger and thirst for righteousness, for they shall be satisfied' (Matthew 5:6 NASB).

Paul tells us in Romans 13:14 (NASB) to 'put on the Lord Jesus Christ, and make no provision for the flesh in regard to its lusts.' The Greek term translated *make… provision* basically refers to caring for, being concerned about, and taking thought for.[6] We are not to think of or do anything that would support or tend to build up the flesh's sinful desires. Letting our thoughts dwell on negative things or immoral subjects can stir up fleshly attitudes of anger, envy, bitterness, and despair and lead to immoral actions. If we just try to avoid thinking wrong thoughts, however, we will usually end up defeated. Instead, we have to think right thoughts. We are to overcome the lie by choosing the truth. Just renouncing the lie will not help us.

Avoid Fleshly Situations

If we want to avoid opening doors to the desires of the flesh, we need to avoid situations and entanglements that can stimulate fleshly behaviour. Having a hidden bottle of alcohol or a secret stash of pornographic magazines somewhere in your room is making provision for the flesh. We make provision as well when we entertain thoughts or make plans for when the deeds of the flesh can be carried out in secret. Paul told young Timothy, 'Flee the evil desires of youth, and pursue righteousness, faith, love and peace, along with those who call on the Lord out of a pure heart. Don't have anything to do with foolish and stupid arguments, because you know they produce quarrels' (2 Timothy 2:22,23).

We are to pursue the things of the Spirit in the fellowship of others. Fellowship with others is important because we're more vulnerable to sin when we are alone. One way to help you not make provision for the flesh is to stay in ongoing fellowship with other believers.

Coming Up Higher

Read

1 Corinthians 9:24–27; Ephesians 6:10–16; Romans 7:25 – 8:2; Galatians 5:16; 1 Peter 2:11.

Reflect

Whether we like it or not, we are in a battle against evil forces. At the cross, Christ won the battle over the power of sin, but the defeated enemies have not yet been totally removed. In a real sense, the battleground is our lives. What images of the Christian life does Paul use in the following verses?

- 1 Timothy 6:11,12

- 2 Timothy 2:3; 4:7

What does the Bible mean when it talks about the 'flesh'?

If the flesh has been crucified why do we still have trouble with it?

When did you first realise you were powerless against sin without Christ? How does the Spirit help you in your struggles?

What do you do in your daily life to take every thought captive to the obedience of Christ (see 2 Corinthians 10:5)?

Respond

Awesome God, I know that in You ultimate victory is certain, but I am very aware that the battle rages now. You, Creator God, know the flesh. You know the temptation I face to enthrone myself and live autonomously. Thank You for providing Your Spirit as a source of strength for me. Teach me to rely on Him. Thank You for providing Your Word as a source of truth as I seek the things above. Help me become a stronger student of the Word. And thank You for providing the body of believers who strengthen me for the battle. In Jesus' name I pray, amen.

To resist the devil is to commit oneself to follow God or to draw near.[1]

— *Peter Davids*

9

Warfare!

Dear Dr Anderson and Mr Park,

Hi, my name is London. I am a few days short of fifteen years old. I just wanted to thank you so much for writing *Bondage Breaker, Youth Edition*.

For a while, I struggled with extreme insecurity, and I felt no one loved me. When I discovered that wasn't true, I would act depressed so I would get attention. I acted this way so much that it became a part of me, in a sense. I went to my youth pastor about the issue. He introduced me to the concept of spiritual warfare. He told me that I didn't have to accept the lies of the enemy since I was a child of God and that I needed to fight back. For a while I would, but the issue would come right back. I would embrace and believe the lies, hence choosing to stay in my rut. I was on a roller coaster. I chose not to believe the truth out of my so-called comfort. My depression felt like a part of me.

About a month ago the warfare got so bad that I went the wrong direction and stopped going to church. I totally avoided my youth pastor and God.

One night, I had to get out of my house and away from my thoughts so I went to church. My youth pastor confronted me out of love, and he recommended that I read *Bondage Breaker, Youth Edition*.

A week later I was in his office again, struggling with the same old stuff. I told him that I had basically cut off my prayer life. At the end of the appointment, he had me pray out loud, myself. It was hard to do, but there was a breakthrough! I finished your book, and I realise now that I need to know the truth for myself. Things are clicking in my spirit. I have to choose the truth. The Spirit will guide me into all truth, which will set me free! I love reading the statements of truth in your book. Thank you so much! Thank God for His mercy! I'm finding that I want to pray and worship God out loud. Hallelujah!

Your sis in Christ,
London.

That is just one of hundreds of unsolicited letters we have received from young people who have truly submitted to God and resisted the devil by using biblical principles and the 'Steps to Freedom in Christ' (a tool that helps people resolve personal and spiritual conflicts that keep them from enjoying a vibrant relationship with God).[2] Christ sets you free, and *what* sets you free is your response to Him in repentance and faith. (We looked at the other two enemies, the flesh and the world, in the previous chapter.)

Engaged in a Real Battle

The one who lies behind and utilises both the world and the flesh in his opposition against the plan of God is 'the ruler of this world' (John 14:30 NASB), the 'prince of the power of the air' (Ephesians 2:2 NASB). John says, 'We know that we are children of God, and that the whole world is under the control of the evil one' (1 John 5:19).

Unfortunately, many Christians aren't aware of that. They don't know who they are in Christ nor why that is even important to know. And there are Christians who don't know in a practical sense that 'our struggle is not against flesh and blood, but against the rulers, against the authorities, against the powers of this dark world and against the spiritual forces of evil in the heavenly realms' (Ephesians 6:12).

The real battle is between Christ and the Antichrist; between the One who is the truth and the father of lies; between the kingdom of light and the kingdom of darkness; between the Spirit of truth and deceiving spirits; and, ultimately, between life and death. Many students will never receive the abundant life that Jesus offers because 'the god of this age has blinded the minds of unbelievers, so that they cannot see the light of the gospel of the glory of Christ, who is the image of God' (2 Corinthians 4:4).

Acknowledging a Real Enemy

That Christians believe in a personal devil has always been part of the doctrinal statement of the historical church. In the beginning of time Satan deceived Eve by his craftiness (see 2 Corinthians 11:3), and in the last days he will continue to be our key adversary (according to the book of Revelation). The reality of this enemy is seen in Peter's words: 'Your enemy the devil prowls around like a roaring lion looking for someone to devour' (1 Peter 5:8). Satan's goal is to 'devour' believers. Just before Jesus was arrested and crucified, He warned Peter, 'Simon, Simon, Satan has asked to sift you as wheat' (Luke

22:31). Through the events up to and following the cross, Satan was going to try to destroy the faith of the disciples (we know this because the word *you* in Luke 22:31 is plural, referring to all of the disciples — not just Peter). Satan hoped that they, like Judas, would be blown away like chaff.[3]

Satan's opposition to God and His children is evident in the names and descriptions ascribed to him. In addition to the name *devil* which means 'slanderer', this chief enemy is known as *Satan*, which means 'adversary'. His character is also evident in the names *the evil one*, *the great dragon* (a terrible monster), and *serpent*, which symbolises his cunning and seducing deceitfulness.

Satan's Schemes

Temptation Through Deception

Although the devil is called 'the tempter' in only two instances (Matthew 4:3; 1 Thessalonians 3:5)[4], he is identified as being related to all temptation when Jesus taught His model prayer: 'And lead us not into temptation [temptation that would overpower us], but deliver us from the evil one' (Matthew 6:13).[5] Every believer has to face and overcome the tempter. It *is* possible to overcome him, according to 1 Corinthians 10:13: 'No temptation has seized you except what is common to man. And God is faithful; he will not let you be tempted beyond what you can bear. But when you are tempted, he will also provide a way out so that you can stand up under it.'

In our book *Radical Image*, we mentioned that true life and growth come from incorporating God's life into our lives via faith in His Word, His truth. The opposite of that is also true: Death and destruction come from that which opposes God — the lie. If we are sanctified by faith as the Holy Spirit leads us into all truth, then Satan's primary strategy for destroying mankind is to counter God's truth with lies. He knows that people will not always live according to what they *profess*, but by what they choose to *believe in their hearts* — just like London expressed in her letter at the start of this chapter.

All temptation is an attempt to get us to live independently of God.

Satan can succeed in leading people away from God and away from His righteous principles by getting them to believe a lie. Do you remember Ananias and Sapphira? They sold property because they wanted to give money to help spread the gospel. Although they said they were giving the entire amount to Peter they held back part of it. God struck down Ananias and Sapphira when they lied to the Holy Spirit (see Acts 5:1–11). He wanted to send a strong message to the early church about the danger of giving in to Satan. The devil's primary strategy is to tempt us to believe and consequently live out his lies. That's how he leads us to our destruction.

It Began with a Lie

The first sin was the result of Satan's temptation through a lie (see Genesis 3:4,5). This original lie reveals the nature of his lies: He wants to get us to doubt God's infinite love and goodness. He wants us to believe that God somehow limits our lives and that His will is not best for us. Satan wants us to believe that we can have richer and fuller lives apart from God. In fact, *all* temptation is an attempt to get us to live our lives independently of God.

Jesus, after declaring that it is the truth in Him that breaks the bonds of sin and sets us free, said to those who sought to kill Him, 'You belong to your father, the devil.... He was a murderer from the beginning, not holding to the truth, for there is no truth in him. When he lies, he speaks his native language, for he is a liar and the father of lies' (John 8:44). It's worth noting that murder and all other sins stem from not knowing the truth and choosing to believe a lie.

Deception is the most powerful weapon in Satan's arsenal. Revelation 20 tells us of a time when Satan will be locked up in an abyss for 1,000 years. The reason for this reveals the nature of his attack: Satan is locked up 'to keep him from deceiving the nations any more until the thousand years were ended' (Revelation 20:3). After the 1,000 years are completed, he will be released for a brief time. Again the nature of his work is clear: 'Satan will be released... and will go out to deceive the nations in the four corners of the earth' (20:7,8). No wonder Jesus prayed in His high priestly prayer:

> I have given them your word and the world has hated them, for they are not of the world any more than I am of the world. My prayer is not that you take them out of the world but that you protect them from the evil one.... Sanctify them by the truth; your word is truth. As you sent me into the world, I have sent them into the world. For them I sanctify myself, that they too may be truly sanctified (John 17:14,15,17–19).

A Crafty Enemy

As we might suspect, the enemy's tactic of deceit includes his method of operation. We are to put on the armour of God so that we can stand against the devil's schemes (Ephesians 6:11). The Greek word translated *schemes* refers to cunning and deceit. Satan's attacks do not always come as obvious frontal assaults.[6] His cleverness caused Paul to warn people against being outwitted (or cheated, defrauded) by the devil (2 Corinthians 2:11).

In 2 Corinthians 11:3, Paul refers to the cunning or craftiness of our enemy. Satan is a hunter. He sets traps to see what he can snare; he traps believers through his cunning, deceitful tactics. Satan himself masquerades as an angel of light. It is not surprising, then, if his servants masquerade as servants of righteousness (2 Corinthians 11:14,15).

Unfortunately, there are many types of traps. The most effective ones seem to call on our search for pleasure and escape. For example, according to tradition, this is one way an Eskimo hunter kills a wolf:

> First, the Eskimo coats his knife blade with animal blood and allows it to freeze. He then adds layer after layer of blood until the blade is completely concealed by the frozen blood.
>
> Next, the hunter fixes his knife in the ground with the blade up. When a wolf follows his sensitive nose to the source of the scent and discovers the bait, he licks it, tasting the blood. He begins to lick faster, more and more vigorously, lapping the blade until the keen edge is bare. Feverishly now, harder and harder, he licks the blade in the cold Arctic night. His craving for blood becomes so great that the wolf does not notice the razor sharp sting of the naked blade on his own tongue. Nor does he recognise the instant when his insatiable thirst is being satisfied by his own warm blood. His carnivorous appetite continues to crave more until in the morning light, the wolf is found dead on the snow.

Similarly, we can also get caught in our own cravings. For instance,

> … many kids begin using drugs, drinking alcohol, smoking cigarettes, or engaging in unsafe sexual behaviour for the same reasons that the wolf begins licking the knife blade. It seems safe and delicious at first, but it doesn't satisfy. More and more is desired, leading to a crisis — death.
>
> Don't be fooled by the temptations of sin. Like the wolf, we can get away with it for a while. Eventually, however, its true character is revealed. Sin leads to death and destruction. 'For the wages of sin is death' (Romans 6:23).[7]

The moment we give in to temptation, Satan immediately changes his strategy and becomes the accuser. He is specifically called 'the accuser of our brothers, who accuses them before our God day and night' (Revelation 12:10). Although that verse speaks of accusations brought before God (as in Job's case — see Job 1:6–12; 2:1–5), Satan also hurls accusations at us via our thoughts in order to beset us with discouragement and depression.

Satan's schemes are more dangerous than we realise because, in his superhuman knowledge, he knows where each of us is prone to sin and uses that knowledge to his advantage. He tempts us to sin through a wide variety of means. Rarely does he expose his hand, and seldom does he attack in an obvious way. His demons come out in darkness and scurry for cover when God's light shines. Satan and his minions' activities are far more covert than overt.

Temptation Through the World System

The approach Satan used to tempt Jesus shows that many of Satan's temptations are handled through others in the world around us. Just before the beginning of Jesus' public ministry, Satan directly assaulted Jesus in the wilderness. Afterwards, 'when the devil had finished all this tempting, he left [Jesus] until an opportune time' (Luke 4:13). Apparently Satan continued to tempt Jesus when favourable opportunities arose. And because there are no other Scripture references that say Satan directly tempted Jesus, we can assume that some of those temptations came through other means. No doubt they included the questions Jesus' enemies asked in an effort to trap Him (Luke 20:20) and Peter's attempt to discourage Jesus from going to the cross (which Jesus saw as inspired by Satan [Matthew 16:21–23]). Most likely those temptations included the struggle Jesus endured in Gethsemane when He was faced with suffering on the cross. Jesus' concern over the possibility that His disciples would be tempted in that hour, no doubt, also applied to

Himself. In all of those situations and more, Jesus was presented with a way to do something that would be easy and pleasing to Him and the world rather than doing the will of His Father. He was 'tempted in every way, just as we are' (Hebrews 4:15).

The devil's involvement in temptations that originate from other people or sources is clearly seen in James' caution:

> If you harbour bitter envy and selfish ambition in your hearts, do not boast about it or deny the truth. Such 'wisdom' does not come down from heaven but is earthly, unspiritual, of the devil. For where you have envy and selfish ambition [or strife], there you find disorder and every evil practice (James 3:14–16).

We can't escape James' point that the lies coming from the god of this world are the cause of envy, selfish ambition, and strife — all of which affect our relationships with other people. Remember what we learned earlier in chapter one? Our emotions are primarily a product of our thoughts.

James' rebuke against worldliness and pride, which evidently brought about slander and sinful judgement of believer against believer, is also clearly related to the devil (James 4:1–12). In James 4:6,7 and 1 Peter 5:6–8, the devil and pride are mentioned together. Satan's temptation of believers by using other people is also clear in his manipulating of other people to persecute others. Peter's warning about the devil, who seeks to devour believers, is given to believers who were enduring suffering through persecution: 'Resist him, standing firm in the faith, because you know that your brothers throughout the world are undergoing the same kind of sufferings' (1 Peter 5:9). The apostle John adds, 'The devil will put some of you in prison to test you, and you will suffer persecution' (Revelation 2:10).

When you talk to Christians who have been victimised by godless people, you will find that many of them, as a result of their persecution, struggle with thoughts that question the existence or care of Jesus, our Lord. Whether through physical pain or various forms of emotional hurt, the devil will tempt us to deny or distrust God, and he will do this through persecution.

Deception Through Direct Thoughts

The Bible also reveals that Satan deceives us by putting certain thoughts in our minds. For example, in the Old Testament we read that 'Satan rose up against Israel and incited David to take a census of Israel' (1 Chronicles 21:1). David went ahead and counted the Israelites even though Joab protested and pointed out that to do so was sin. Although David later confessed that he had done wrong, 70,000 men of Israel still died as a result of his sin.

In John 13:2 we read that the devil had prompted Judas Iscariot to betray Jesus. We may be tempted to dismiss Judas' betrayal as just a bad decision that came from the flesh, but Scripture clearly says that his thoughts about betraying Jesus originated from Satan. When Judas realised what he had done, he took his own life. That affirms the end result of all that Satan does: 'The thief comes only to steal and kill and destroy' (John 10:10).

In relation to the devil and our thoughts, Martin Luther said, 'The devil throws hideous thoughts into the soul — hatred of God, blasphemy and despair.' We (Neil and Dave) have counselled hundreds of students who experienced struggles in their thought lives. Some young people had difficulty concentrating on and reading their Bibles, while others actually heard 'voices' or struggled with accusing and condemning thoughts. With few exceptions, those thoughts were proved to be spiritual battles for the mind.

Deception Through False Teachers

Demons are also behind false teachings that lead believers from the truth. Paul wrote in 1 Timothy 4:1, 'The Spirit clearly says that in later times some will abandon the faith and follow deceiving spirits and things taught by demons.' He then added that such demonic teaching comes through human teachers. Similarly, those who oppose the truth and are involved in false teachings are said to be in 'the trap of the devil' (2 Timothy 2:26).

It is possible that Paul viewed evil spirits as being behind legalistic teachings that held people in bondage. In Colossians 2:8 he warned, 'See to it that no one takes you captive through hollow and deceptive philosophy, which depends on human tradition and the basic principles of this world rather than on Christ.' (See also Galatians 4:9.) In other words, the teachings of these 'spiritual confidence tricksters' were really 'a tool in the hands of... demonic personal forces.' Peter also warned that 'there were also false prophets among the people, just as there will be false teachers among you' (2 Peter 2:1). John said it is our responsibility to test the spirits:

> Dear friends, do not believe every spirit, but test the spirits to see whether they are from God, because many false prophets have gone out into the world.... They are from the world and therefore speak from the viewpoint of the world, and the world listens to them (1 John 4:1,5).

Notice that we aren't to test the false prophets, but rather test the *spirits* that they are in bondage to. This requires mature spiritual discernment because there are 'false apostles, deceitful workmen, masquerading as apostles of Christ' (2 Corinthians 11:13). One telltale sign that these false prophets sometimes exhibit is that they despise authority (see 2 Peter 2:10).

Three Sources of Temptation

How does Satan's work relate to the attacks of our other enemies, the world and the flesh? Is Satan the cause of our temptations, or is the world, or our own sinful flesh, or is it a combination of these? Scripture reveals that it is difficult, if not impossible, to separate the temptations that arise from these three sources — and to do so may be wrong. We have seen that Satan is the 'god of this age' and 'the prince of this world.' The world is under his control. Something of what this means is seen when the apostle Paul describes Satan as 'the spirit who is now at work in those who are disobedient'[8] — that is, those who follow 'the ways of this world' (Ephesians 2:2).

What is significant is that the Greek word for *works in*, which describes Satan's activity in those in the world, is the same word used to speak of God's working in His people. In fact, whenever the agent of the *working* is directly stated, it is either divine or satanic — most often the former (see also Ephesians 1:11,19). By using both the words *spirit* and *work in* in Ephesians 2:2, Paul seems to be purposefully suggesting a rivalry between the satanic spirit and God's Spirit.[9]

An interesting use of *works in* also appears in Philippians 2:13: 'for it is God who works in you [believers] to will and to act according to his good purpose.' Without suggesting that evil spirits indwell unbelievers in exactly the way that the Holy Spirit indwells believers, Paul seems to be saying that those who are dominated by the world are also under the powerful influence of Satan and demons.[10]

After talking about the satanic inspiration of the world system in the first two verses of Ephesians 2, Paul shows how that relates to the flesh. Describing us before our salvation, Paul says, 'We too all formerly lived in the lusts of our flesh, indulging the desires of the flesh' (verse 3 NASB). In other words, walking according to the world system is the same as living according to the desires and passions of the flesh. The propensities of the flesh to find life apart from God are the very things that the world system values and lures the flesh to go after. Thus, according to Ephesians 2:2, the world and the flesh operate 'according to the prince of the power of the air, of the spirit that is now working in the sons of disobedience.'

A similar relationship of the flesh, the world, and the demonic is seen in the epistle of James. In chapter 1, James points to the origin of our sin as following the temptation of the flesh: 'Each one is tempted when, by his own evil desire [of the flesh], he is dragged away and enticed. Then, after desire has conceived, it gives birth to sin' (verses 14,15). Later James reveals that demonic powers lie behind our personal evil desires. The 'wisdom' that promotes the fleshly acts of bitter envy, selfish ambition, disorder, and every evil practice' is ultimately 'of the devil' or demonic in origin (see James 3:14–16). Finally, when James warns against friendship with the world, his cure is to 'resist the devil' (4:4–7). Again the world, the satanic, and the flesh are all tied together in our battle with the power of sin.[11]

All three of our enemies are involved in temptation's pull for us to live apart from God. Satan utilises the power of sin (which also controls him) to control mankind, thus forming a world system structured on values opposed to God's principles of righteousness. He then uses this worldly system, which surrounds and confronts all people, to pull at the old ways of the flesh that still linger in each believer — ways that are oriented towards worldly values.

Who Is Ultimately Responsible?

Even though three enemies are involved in attempting to pull us away from God, it is important to note that the final responsibility for our sin rests on us. No one can say 'the devil made me do it' or 'the attraction of the world was too powerful; I couldn't help myself.' God *always* provides a way of escape for us (see 1 Corinthians 10:13). We are the agents of our own choice to sin.

Despite the flesh, the world, and the underlying powerful influence of the god of this world, those who choose to sin are credited with responsibility for their actions: '*You* were dead in *your* trespasses and sins... *you* formerly walked according to the course of this world.... We too all formerly *lived* [actively 'walked'] in the lusts of *our* flesh... ' (Ephesians 2:1–3 NASB, emphasis added). In the same way, James says that despite the world and the devil, sin is born when 'each one...is carried away and enticed by *his own lust*' (James 1:14 NASB, emphasis added). Satan filled the heart of Ananias to lie, but Peter asked him, 'Why is it that *you* have conceived this deed in your heart?' (Acts 5:4 NASB, emphasis added).

This, of course, does not necessarily mean that all sinful thoughts originate within us. If it's true that Satan can plant thoughts in our minds, then their original source is alien. But when those thoughts result in sin, they become ours. They become our own fleshly thoughts that we've allowed to turn into a desire that issues in a sinful act. As believers in Christ, we are indwelt by the Spirit of God and freed from the bondage of sin. We must make the responsible choice to serve our Lord rather than give in to the temptations to sin.

The Extent of Satan's Attacks

We as Christians are no longer in the kingdom of darkness and Satan's power has been broken, but we can still enslave ourselves by the choices we make. The Bible teaches that we have been delivered from Satan's power just as we have been delivered from sin's power (see Acts 26:18; Colossians 1:12,13). Our Saviour has already defeated the god of this world and all the evil spiritual powers (see John 12:31; 16:11; Colossians 2:15). We have been joined to Christ in the heavenly realm, where He is 'far above all rule and authority, power and dominion' (Ephesians 1:21). We are completely equipped to wage victorious warfare against Satan and all of his evil spiritual forces (see Ephesians 6:11–18). Nothing, including demons, can separate us from the love of God that is in Christ Jesus our Lord (Romans 8:38,39). Listen to how Eugene Peterson says it in his account of Romans from *The Message*:

> So, what do you think? With God on our side like this, how can we lose? If God didn't hesitate to put everything

on the line for us, embracing our condition and exposing himself to the worst by sending his own Son, is there anything else he wouldn't gladly and freely do for us? And who would dare tangle with God by messing with one of God's chosen? Who would dare even to point a finger? The One who died for us — who raised to live for us! — is in the presence of God at this very moment sticking up for us. Do you think anyone is going to be able to drive a wedge between us and Christ's love for us? There is no way! Not trouble, not hard times, not hatred, not hunger, not homelessness, not bullying threats, not backstabbing, not even the worst sins listed in Scripture:

'They kill us in cold blood because they hate you. We're sitting ducks; they pick us off one by one.'

None of this fazes us because Jesus loves us. I'm absolutely convinced that nothing — nothing living or dead, angelic or demonic, today or tomorrow, high or low, thinkable or unthinkable — absolutely *nothing* can get between us and God's love because of the way that Jesus our Master has embraced us.

Opening Ourselves to Satan's Influence

Having said all this, however, Scripture indicates that believers can still give themselves over to sin and evil powers and become enslaved to them. The Bible clearly states that our freedom is real, but we are commanded to make it real in our life experiences. That happens when we exercise, through faith in God's truth, what is ours in Christ. We are no longer slaves, but we can still choose to live like one.

Paul warned us to avoid letting sin reign in our mortal bodies by using our bodies as instruments of unrighteousness (see Romans 6:12–23). This and other portions of Scripture affirm that we can allow Satan and demons to exert their influence upon us. This influence can have a varied extent of control over us, but it cannot separate us from the love of God — nor keep us from being the person He created us to be.

The basic biblical picture of man is that he is open to outside influence, which is ultimately either from God or evil spirits. The soul was never designed to function as its own master; we will either serve God or money (Matthew 6:24). Jesus and those who wrote the Scriptures viewed man as being vulnerable to external supernatural forces.

Scripture reveals that believers can, in different ways, come under the influence of Satan and demons. For instance, in 2 Corinthians 2:10,11 we are urged to forgive because we are not ignorant of Satan's schemes.

Even Christians Need to Be Ready!

Paul's hope for those who oppose the Lord's servants is that God would 'grant them repentance leading them to a knowledge of the truth, and that they will come to their senses and escape from the trap of the devil, who has taken them captive to do his will' (2 Timothy 2:25,26). To apply this passage to the unsaved only is to miss the point of the epistle and deny that Christians, even good ones, can be deceived.

The possibility that a believer can be trapped by the evil one is seen in 1 Timothy 3, where Paul lists the qualifications of a church leader: He is to have 'a good reputation with outsiders, so that he will not fall into disgrace and into the devil's trap' (verse 7).

—————————— Check it out! ——————————

*The trap is one set **by** the devil, not **for** him.*

As the verse above indicates, those held captive need to come back to their senses. A person without a good testimony from outsiders could '"lose his head" or "senses" when he fell into reproach and be ensnared to obey the evil one and disobey God.'[12]

That believers can be influenced is seen in these words from Paul: '"In your anger do not sin": Do not let the sun go down while you are still angry, and do not give the devil a foothold' (Ephesians 4:26,27). The word *foothold* literally means 'a place'. Clearly, a believer's sin is not simply a matter of the flesh; it is also that of the devil as well.

Correctly Responding to Satanic Attacks

Repenting of Our Sins

If we find that we have succumbed to Satan's influence, our first response has to be repentance, as Paul indicated in 2 Timothy 2:25,26 NASB: 'The Lord's bond-servant must... with gentleness [correct] those who are in opposition, if perhaps God may grant them repentance leading to the knowledge of the truth, and they may come to their senses and escape from the snare of the devil, having been held captive by him to do his will.'

—————————— Check It Out! ——————————

The critical issue is our relationship with God.

An unrepentant person is like a house in which the rubbish has piled up for months. That is going to attract a lot of flies. The primary answer, however, is not to get rid of the flies, but rather, the rubbish. It's not necessary for us to study the flight patterns of the flies or determine their names and rank structure. The answer has been and always will be repentance and faith in God.[13]

Taking a Stand in the Faith

When we're faced with satanic attacks, the critical issue is our relationship with God. Once that is established, we can stand against the evil one. 'Submit yourselves, then, to God: Resist the devil, and he will flee from you' (James 4:7). 'Be self-controlled and alert. Your enemy the devil prowls around like a roaring lion looking for someone to devour. Resist him, standing firm in the faith' (1 Peter 5:8,9). The Greek word for *resist* in both verses is literally 'stand against'. We are to take our stand in Christ against the devil and his demons.

Standing firm in the faith is not so much a matter of holding to true doctrine, but rather it's more of a 'personal or communal commitment.'[14] 'A flint-like resolution is what [Peter] calls for here.'[15] There is no place for passivity or being a wimp in the Christian walk. We must actively take our place in Christ. We cannot passively put on the armour of God:

> Therefore *put on* the full armour of God, so that when the day of evil comes, you may be able to stand your ground, and after you have done everything, to stand. Stand firm then, with the belt of truth buckled around your waist, with the breastplate of righteousness in place, and with your feet fitted with the readiness that comes from the gospel of peace (Ephesians 6:13–15, emphasis added).

In Romans 13, putting on the 'armour of light' is the same as putting on the Lord Jesus Christ (see verses 13,14). *The only sanctuary we have is in Christ.*

Choosing the Truth

Like London, the girl in the opening letter in this chapter, we need to *choose truth*. This is our first line of defence. 'We take captive every thought to make it obedient to Christ' (2 Corinthians 10:5). We're not supposed to try to analyse whether a thought came from the television set, another person, our own memories, or from the pit. We are to take *every thought* captive. Does that mean we should rebuke every negative thought? No, because we would be doing that for the rest of our lives.

Instead, we are to overcome the father of lies by choosing the truth. We are not called to dispel the darkness; we are called to turn on the light.

Making Ourselves Humble

Commitment to God means making ourselves low before Him. Both James 4:6 and 1 Peter 5:5 say, 'God opposes the proud but gives grace to the humble.' Humility is confidence properly placed. Like Paul, we should 'put no confidence in the flesh' (Philippians 3:3); rather, we should place all our confidence in God. Pride makes us vulnerable to the devil.

The command that we are to *resist* the devil means we should not be out looking for Satan to engage him in hostile action. We should never let the devil set the agenda because the Holy Spirit is our guide. We are to 'be self-controlled and alert' (1 Peter 5:8). We are to be aware of Satan's schemes (2 Corinthians 2:11). Ignorance is not bliss; it is defeat.

Arming Ourselves

Warfare against a spiritual foe requires spiritual weapons. Paul says, 'The weapons we fight with are not the weapons of the world. On the contrary, they have divine power to demolish strongholds' (2 Corinthians 10:4). We are also told to 'put on the full armour of God' (Ephesians 6:11). The Lord Himself used only spiritual weapons (the Word of God) against the devil. We can stand against the power of Satan only by the power of the One who has overcome him — Christ Jesus. Thus, abiding in Christ and walking by the Spirit are required for victory in spiritual warfare against the demonic enemy.

Spiritual warfare rests on immediate communion with God for fresh power. When we are watchful, resisting the devil, and fighting with spiritual weapons, we are also to be praying for God's help: 'Lead us not into temptation, but deliver us from the evil one' (Matthew 6:13). In the same way, Paul finished his words about standing against the enemy with God's armour by saying, 'Pray in the Spirit on all occasions with all kinds of prayers and requests. With this in mind, be alert and always keep on praying for all the saints' (Ephesians 6:18).

Victory Is Assured

Do you know that Satan's attacks have limitations? He can do only what God permits (see Job 1:11,12; 2:3–5; Luke 22:31). 'The battle is the LORD's' (1 Samuel 17:47). Battling Satan is not our personal fight. It is part of an ongoing war between good and evil. And we are led by the Unconquerable One, who has already won the decisive battle. Christ said, 'Take heart! I have overcome the world' (John 16:33). In praise, Paul exclaimed, 'Thanks be to God! He gives us the victory through our Lord Jesus Christ' (1 Corinthians 15:57).

Coming Up Higher

Read

John 14:30; Ephesians 6:12; 2 Corinthians 4:4; 1 Peter 5:8; 1 Corinthians 10:13; Matthew 4:1–11.

Reflect

The flesh and the world are two enemies of sanctification. What is the third and ultimate enemy?

The one who lies behind and uses both the world and the flesh is Satan. What does John 14:30 call him and how does Ephesians 6:12 identify him?

What does Ephesians 6:12 teach about the nature of the battle believers face in this life?

What battles do you face at home? School? With friends?

According to 2 Corinthians 4:4 why do some people never receive the abundant life that Jesus offered?

Even though we face three enemies it is still our responsibility to say no to sin. What tools does God give to us as believers to overcome these enemies?

What promise do you find in 1 Corinthians 10:13?

Respond

Almighty God, this chapter has reminded me that, as Your child, I am engaged in a real spiritual battle. From experience, I know all too well Satan's efforts to deceive and his strategies of deception. So I find great hope in Your promise to help me overcome when I'm tempted. In order to stand against Satan, I ask You to help me acknowledge, confess, and repent of my sins. Give me the ability to recognise and choose truth. Help me place my confidence in You, not in myself. Thank You that I can rest in the truth that victory is assured in Christ. In Jesus' name I pray, amen.

God whispers to us in our pleasures,
speaks in our conscience, but shouts
in our pains.[1]

— *C. S. Lewis*

When the Going Gets Tough

Have you ever felt like nothing was going right? Everyone has felt that way from time to time because that's life. It can be like the young man who was learning to be a paratrooper:

Before his first jump, he was given these instructions:

1. Jump when you are told.
2. Count to ten and pull the ripcord.
3. In the unlikely event your parachute doesn't open, pull the emergency ripcord.
4. When you get down, a truck will be there to take you back to the airport.

The young man memorised these instructions and climbed aboard the plane. The plane climbed to 10,000 feet and the paratroopers began to jump. When the young man was told to jump, he jumped. He then counted to ten and pulled the ripcord. Nothing happened. His chute failed to open. So he pulled the emergency ripcord. Still nothing happened. No parachute.

'Oh great,' said the young man. 'And I suppose the truck won't be there when I get down either!'[2]

Have you ever felt like that guy? Sometimes it feels like we have so many failures and disappointments in life that we just don't expect anything to go right ever again. But remember: Sometimes God gives us specific trials to help us become more like Jesus. In the face of a trial we may be tempted to lose hope, but God is always with us. We are to put our hope in Him. God tests our faith for a purpose. He is testing us so that our hope comes alive and we learn to trust in Him. But how do we know if we are putting our hope in God? Practising the Christian life begins with being a good steward of everything God has entrusted to us, including our own lives. Of course, we can commit to God only what we know about ourselves, which is not everything there is to know. Paul says in 1 Corinthians 4:1–5 NASB:

> Let a man regard us in this manner, as servants of Christ, and stewards of the mysteries of God. In this case, moreover, it is required of stewards that one be found trustworthy. But to me it is a very small thing that I should be examined by you, or by any human court; in fact, I do not even examine myself. For I am conscious of nothing against myself, yet I am not by this acquitted; but the one who examines me is the Lord. Therefore do not go on passing judgement before the time, but wait until the Lord comes who will both bring to light the things hidden in the darkness and disclose the motives of men's hearts; and then each man's praise will come to him from God.

This passage, which tells us that God will reveal our hearts at the final judgement on the 'day of the Lord,' clearly reveals that we don't have total knowledge of ourselves. Other Bible passages also show that the revealing of our hearts takes place not only at the last day, but also in our present lives. The psalmist prayed, 'Search me, O God, and know my heart; test me and know my anxious thoughts. See if there is any offensive way in me, and lead me in the way everlasting' (Psalm 139:23,24). The Word of God also reveals people's hearts:

> The word of God is living and active. Sharper than any double-edged sword, it penetrates even to dividing soul and spirit, joints and marrow; it judges the thoughts and attitudes of the heart. Nothing in all creation is hidden from God's sight. Everything is uncovered and laid bare before the eyes of him to whom we must give account (Hebrews 4:12,13).

Growing up includes the process of God revealing to us unconscious thoughts or the unconscious contents of the heart.

Growth and Transparency

We can divide the Christian into four parts as follows (as we discuss this diagram, keep in mind that we are talking about *character — who* we are rather than *what* we do):

In all of us there's a part that is totally transparent, the part of our lives that we know all about — and so does the rest of the world. Then there is a part of us that we know but don't want others to know. Let's suppose someone recognises a Hollywood celebrity, Harrison Ford, as he steps into a lift. The person asks, 'Are you the real Indiana Jones — I mean Harrison Ford?' As the lift doors close, Ford responds, 'Only when I'm alone.' Just as the celebrity has a hidden side that no one knows, we too have hidden sides. There are some things about ourselves we just don't want to share with others. What keeps us from being

	You see	**You don't see**
I see	Transparent self	Pride
I don't see	Blind spots	Hidden self

totally transparent people? Probably the fear of rejection, or perhaps our pride is involved. Whatever the case, we usually try to project an image of ourselves that is more positive and perfect than who we really are.

Our Christian growth will always be hindered to the degree that we cover up who we really are. That's because we get wrapped up in how we look to other people rather than who we are to God. God calls us to 'walk in the light as He Himself is in the light' (1 John 1:7 NASB). He wants us to put aside lies and speak the truth with our friends because we are members of one another (see Ephesians 4:25). 'Speaking the truth in love, we are to grow up in all aspects into Him, who is the head, even Christ' (Ephesians 4:15 NASB). Every Christian should make a real effort to live this way in every area of his or her life, at school and at home.

We are conscious of everything above the middle line in the diagram but there are some things below the line that others know, yet we aren't even aware of. These are our blind spots (and we all have them). It doesn't take a genius to see the character defects in other people. But we are not supposed to judge other people's characters; in fact, we are commanded not to. We are supposed to accept one another as Christ has accepted us. Nothing frees a person more for growth than the unconditional love and acceptance of others. However, *don't confuse judgement with discipline*. There is a difference: Discipline is always based on observed behaviour; judgement is always related to character.

The last part in the diagram is that which only God knows. He has total knowledge of us — He even knows how many hairs we have on our heads. Now, let's tie all this together as it relates to Christian growth. Take a look at the following diagram.

As we noted previously, Paul said there are times when we can say, 'It is a very small thing that I should be examined by you, or by any human court; in fact, I do not even examine myself. I am conscious of nothing against myself, yet I am not by this acquitted; but the one who examines me is the Lord' (1 Corinthians 4:3–5 NASB). Paul is saying that we shouldn't be concerned about what others think of us because the One who examines us is the Lord. Paul had already examined himself and knew of nothing against himself. To his knowledge, he had no unresolved conflicts. He had nothing more to confess, and there

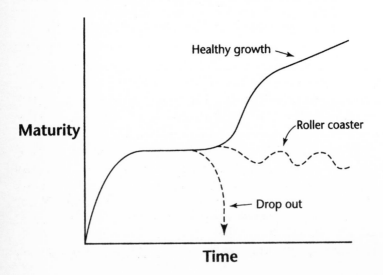

was nobody he needed to forgive or ask forgiveness of. Even in light of all that, he still said that he was 'not by this acquitted.' Although he had at that point reached a plateau in his Christian walk (as we all do at times), he knew he still hadn't arrived. These plateaus are the good times in the process of being sanctified. We don't feel convicted by anything and our consciences are clean.

Growth and Suffering

No plateau, however, lasts forever. God has a way of letting us know that we are not yet qualified to be a member of the Trinity! Usually the way we interact with people reveals how stubborn and immature we really are. The Lord is clearly involved in reproving us: 'Whom the LORD loves He reproves' (Proverbs 3:12 NASB). God can also reprove (correct) us when we study His Word: 'All Scripture is inspired by God and profitable for teaching, for reproof, for correction, for training in righteousness' (2 Timothy 3:16 NASB).

--- **Check It Out!** ---

A mistake is never a failure unless you fail to learn from it.

There are three basic responses to the corrections of life. One option is to drop out. Dropouts skip youth group because they don't want to hear the truth. They don't want to be convicted, nor do they want to change themselves or their lifestyles. So they stay away from anything that might make them feel guilty.

Another option is to hang in there but never grow up. This is the classic roller-coaster Christian. To this believer, God may appear to be saying, 'You didn't learn from that experience, so I will have to take you through that again. You still didn't learn? I'll take you through the situation again. You still didn't learn? Through the situation again... and again... and again....'

What should we do when we find ourselves falling short of

the glory of God? That brings us to our third option: Own up to your 'something less than Christlike character.' When you realise that you reacted to someone impatiently or unkindly, admit it. Don't blame someone else or rationalise your attitude or behaviour. Just walk in the light by agreeing with God that perfection has still escaped you. Admit what you did, apologise, ask for forgiveness, forgive or do whatever Scripture requires you to do, and most important of all, be honest with God and the people around you. A mistake is never a failure unless you fail to learn from it. Someone once said that to stumble and fall is not failure. Even if you stumble and fall again, that is not failure. Failure comes when you say you were pushed when you weren't. In other words, the corrections of life don't cause us to fail; they just reveal who we really are. A huge power failure that involved much of the northeast United States in November 1965 helps us to understand the importance of character and perseverance.

> At 5.18 pm New York City went black, as well as much of the entire state. The affected area covered some 80,000 square miles and took in most of seven U.S. states and most of Canada's province of Ontario. Whether it was a generator feeding power at the wrong frequency or a switch thrown in error by some utility company employee was hard to determine.
>
> But the millions of people living in New York and the surrounding area quickly determined that they were without electricity. The lights were out, the power was out, and many were stuck for the night in subway train stations, lifts, and tunnels under the East River.
>
> The blackout left some 200 planes in the air above New York's Kennedy International Airport. They had to be rerouted to airports in other states where runway lights were still burning. Overall loss in business due to the blackout, which lasted in some areas up to thirteen hours, was estimated at $100 million dollars. A tyre company, for example, lost $50,000 worth of tyres when power

failed during a critical curing process. A car manufacturer had to throw away fifty engine blocks because high-speed drills froze while boring piston holes. Bakeries in New York alone reported a loss of 300,000 loaves of bread, which were spoiled when the power went off.

All in all, modern civilisation as Americans and Canadians knew it came to a screeching halt that November night because the power supply on which they were dependent had been cut off.

The Christian, too, has a power supply on which he is completely dependent. As John 16:8–15 points out, the Holy Spirit is our power. The Holy Spirit not only does the job of convicting and convincing the world of sin and showing us our blind spots, He also leads us, guides us, and empowers us. But when we cut off the current by quenching the Holy Spirit, his activity ceases and we are living in the flesh. Just as New Yorkers groped around in darkened subways and tunnels under the East River on the night of the biggest blackout they ever experienced, the Christian who dims the power of the Holy Spirit in his life walks about in spiritual weakness. But unlike the victims of the 1965 power failure, we don't need to wait for someone else to turn the power back on. All we have to do is throw the switches marked faith and obedience, and the spiritual lights will go on again.[3]

God's Design in Suffering

Paul's attitude towards the trials and tribulations of life is seen in Romans 5:3–5 NASB: 'We also exult in our tribulations, knowing that tribulation brings about perseverance; and perseverance, proven character; and proven character, hope; and hope does not disappoint, because the love of God has been poured out within our hearts through the Holy Spirit who was given to us.'

We have a God of hope. Unfortunately, people have a tendency to say, 'My parents or job or friends are hopeless,' and they think the solution is to change parents or jobs or friends. What we should do instead is hang in there and grow up! There may be times when it is appropriate for us to change jobs or friends, but if our motivation is to avoid our present trials and tribulations, then the change won't do us any good. Our problems will always follow us no matter where we go.

When we are faced with difficulties, our hope lies in proven character. God's intention is that we come through the trials and tribulations of life a better person than we were before. If we're willing, nothing can keep us from becoming the person that God wants us to be!

The humble way of bringing about this kind of growth is to deny yourself, pick up your cross daily, and follow Him (Matthew 16:24); the key is to do it *daily*. Let us illustrate:

> In Southern California, there are many earthquake faults, like the renowned San Andreas Fault. Because the earth's giant subterranean plates are moving slowly under the crust, we frequently have minor quakes that reflect small adjustments being made along the affected fault lines. They usually shake up the population a little and remind us of God's power or our weakness, but they do very little damage. But in places where the fault lines refuse to adjust to the movements of the subterranean plates, a great amount of pressure is created. Eventually the pressure becomes so great that the fault snaps — creating a large quake. Usually, the longer the pressure has built up, the bigger the earthquake can be.

That's how it is with us as Christians. God has no other plan for us more important than our sanctification. If we fail to grow over time, we may find ourselves brought against a major adjustment that God uses to get our attention. He may go so far as to sacrifice our jobs or achievements if we fail to conform to His image.

The Lord was patient with David after he sinned with

Bathsheba. God gave him at least nine months to own up to his sin. David was under heavy conviction, but he did not acknowledge his sin so the Lord spoke to him through a prophet. The end result? David lost the child he had with Bathsheba. In his hindsight, David's counsel to us is: 'I will instruct you and teach you in the way you should go; I will counsel you and watch over you. Do not be like the horse or the mule, which have no understanding but must be controlled by bit and bridle' (Psalm 32:8,9).

Though many of us may face major adjustments in life at one time or another, these adjustments aren't always easy to see. They're more obvious in extreme cases, such as a young person who is struggling with alcohol. Let's say this teen turned to alcohol as a means of coping with the pressures of life or dealing with physical or emotional pain. This choice shuts down his spiritual growth, and along the way he finds that he needs more and more alcohol as his tolerance level increases. As his life continues to fall apart, he refuses to admit he has a problem. Finally a big adjustment comes. God allows him to lose his health and his after-school job. God knows it won't be enough just to get this person to stop drinking because his spiritual needs have become so great. He has overwhelming needs that only Christ can meet, and he needs to get back on the track of conforming to the image of God.

When Paul corrected the Corinthians for their worldly behaviour, he concluded by saying, 'What do you prefer? Shall I come to you with a whip, or in love and with a gentle spirit?' (1 Corinthians 4:21). If you were a parent, wouldn't you prefer to discipline your children by talking to them rather than having to use a rod (see Proverbs 22:15)? Good parents will not spare the rod if they have to, but most parents, like God, prefer to discipline with love and a spirit of gentleness. When we need to be reproved, do we want God to use a rod or gently discipline us? The choice is ours.

The suffering we face as we grow from sin toward holiness is inevitable. Yet we can take comfort in knowing that one of the great themes of the Bible is glory through suffering. Jesus walked the path of suffering to glory, and so did His disciples. The apostle Paul knew that if he wanted to experience the power of Christ's resurrection as the dynamic force that transformed his life, then he had to endure 'the fellowship of sharing in [Christ's] sufferings, becoming like him in his death' (Philippians 3:10). Paul said to the Colossian believers, 'I fill up in my flesh what is still lacking in regard to Christ's afflictions' (Colossians 1:24). He was saying that his sufferings were part of the measure of sufferings that must be endured *en route* to the final state of perfection. Every believer participates in this great drama of suffering that leads to glory.

Sanctification often involves warfare, and in warfare someone always suffers. Suffering, for the believer, is often related to the cosmic struggle between God and Satan. In this spiritual war, we won't be defeated because we are in Christ. We can have the same attitude as the apostles in the early church, who rejoiced 'because they had been counted worthy of suffering disgrace for the Name' (Acts 5:41).

The Necessity of Suffering

The necessity of suffering is made clear to us in the Bible. We will share in the glory of Christ only if we 'share in his sufferings' (Romans 8:17). If we endure in suffering we will also reign with Him (see 2 Timothy 2:9,10,12). 'Just as the sufferings of Christ flow over into our lives, so also through Christ our comfort overflows' (2 Corinthians 1:5).

Much of the suffering faced by believers is a result of living for Christ in a hostile world. Trials are destined to come in spreading the gospel of Christ and shouldn't be surprising or thought as something strange. Acts 14:22 says, 'we must go through many hardships to enter the kingdom of God.'

As we have already seen, suffering can come in the form of correction from God when we're involved in sin. When David sinned, he felt the heavy hand of God in physical and mental suffering (Psalm 32:3–5). Even apart from sin, our Father will put us through discipline in order to help us grow. Christ, even though He was sinless, was nevertheless perfected through suffering (Hebrews 2:9,10; 5:8).

Our Response to Suffering

Suffering is inevitable. None of us is too crazy about it, but the Bible tells us that we can expect it and, in fact, it is part of our spiritual growth. If we are Christ's disciples, we can expect to be persecuted: 'If they persecuted me, they will persecute you also,' Jesus said (John 15:20). Thus Peter tells the suffering church of his day, 'Do not be surprised at the painful trial you are suffering, as though something strange were happening to you' (1 Peter 4:12). Suffering for the sake of righteousness can't be avoided. Possibly you have heard the following story, but we need to hear it again to help us understand suffering from God's perspective:

> A man found a cocoon of an emperor moth and took it home so he could watch the moth come out of the cocoon. One day a small opening appeared. The man sat and watched the moth for several hours as it struggled to force its body through that little hole. Then it seemed to stop making any progress. To the man it appeared as if the moth had got as far as it could in breaking out of the cocoon and was stuck.
>
> Out of kindness the man decided to help the moth. He took a pair of scissors and snipped off the remaining bit of the cocoon so that the moth could get out. Soon the moth emerged, but it had a swollen body and small shrivelled wings. The man continued to watch the moth, expecting that in time the wings would enlarge and expand to be able to support the body, which would simultaneously contract to its proper size.
>
> Neither happened. In fact, that little moth spent the rest of its life crawling around with a swollen body and shrivelled wings. It was never able to fly.

This man in his kindness and haste didn't understand that the restricting cocoon and the struggle required of the moth to get through the tiny opening were God's way of forcing fluid from the body into the wings so that the moth would be ready to fly once it achieved its freedom from the cocoon.

Just as the moth could only achieve freedom and flight as a result of struggling, we often need to struggle to become all God intends us to be. Sometimes we wish that God would remove our struggles and take away all the obstacles; but just as the man crippled the emperor moth, so we would be crippled if God did that for us. God doesn't take away our problems and difficulties, but He promises to be with us in the midst of them and to use them to restore us, making us into better and stronger people.[4]

We live in a world that is conditioned by sin. The creation from God's good hand was a creation of order and harmony. All the elements of the material and spiritual worlds were in proper relationship. But sin has infected every realm with disorder and improper relationships — and physical, emotional, and spiritual pain are the result. We can expect pain in all three realms, but remember: God is doing something awesome through it all.

Three Key Truths

The Bible tells us that we cannot escape from suffering in this life. 'In fact, everyone who wants to live a godly life in Christ Jesus will be persecuted' (2 Timothy 3:12). The proper response for us, then, is to let suffering work towards our sanctification. We must always view suffering in the light of our loving, heavenly Father. That is made possible when we keep in mind three key truths about suffering.

1. God is always in control of our suffering.

No matter what the source of our suffering — whether directly from God's discipline, from the hand of another person, or simply from the evil that is part of the fallen world — it is under the control of God. In His omniscient wisdom and infinite love, He allows suffering to come our way for His ultimate glory. He allows suffering either for our own transformation or so that He can glorify Himself before other people.

We may never know fully the reasons for all the sufferings we endure in this life. But when we recognise that God uses our suffering for our good or His, we can more easily let suffering contribute to our growth and ultimately to God's perfect glory.

2. God always has a limit on the amount of suffering He allows.

Just as God clearly set limits on the suffering that Satan could bring to Job, so also does He set limits for our suffering (see Job 1:12; 2:6). Some saints, such as Job and Paul, obviously have broader shoulders that enable them to suffer more for righteousness' sake. When we suffer, we're usually tempted to respond either in despondency and say, 'God has forsaken me and there is no hope,' or in anger and say, 'God, I hate You for letting this happen, so I'm forgetting You! I'm going to go my own way from now on.' But our heavenly Father assures us that He will allow no suffering we cannot bear:

> No temptation [testing or trial] has seized you except what is common to man. And God is faithful; he will not let you be tempted beyond what you can bear [beyond your strength]. But when you are tempted, he will also provide a way out so that you can [have strength to] stand up under it (1 Corinthians 10:13).

This promise assures us that God places a limit on our suffering. He knows how much we can bear in each circumstance. He knows the strengths and weaknesses in every area of our lives —

bodily, emotionally, and spiritually. He assures us that He will not allow any suffering (on *any* occasion) that we cannot handle with His grace. We can be confident that the will of God will never take us where the grace of God will not sustain us.

3. God will always provide a way out so that we can stand up under our suffering.

The phrase *stand up under* tells us that God doesn't simply bring about an immediate cessation of the sufferings. What we *can* count on is that God will give us the grace we need to withstand our suffering until it is removed. It is our trust in God's faithfulness and His promise of a way out that gives us the strength to endure suffering.

Nowhere in the Bible are we ever promised that God will keep us from suffering — or remove it quickly when it comes. Rather, He promises to provide grace that enables us faithfully to endure it. The psalmist did not say, 'Cast your cares on the Lord and go free from care,' but rather, 'Cast your cares on the LORD and he will sustain you' (Psalm 55:22). Similarly, Paul does not tell us that the causes of our anxieties will be removed. He says that in their midst we can be garrisoned with God's peace (Philippians 4:6,7). When Paul was in prison and on trial, he testified that the Lord stood at his side and gave him strength (see 2 Timothy 4:17).

─────────────── Check It Out! ───────────────

God is 'the Father of compassion... who comforts us in all our troubles.'

Growth and God's Reward

God makes everything right in the end, yet our reward may not be in this lifetime. We truly believe that when our life on earth is done, all those who have remained faithful will say that the will of God is good, acceptable, and perfect (Romans 12:2).

Suffering is the crucible in which faith and confidence in God are developed. Suffering for the sake of righteousness makes us into the people God wants us to be. To remember the dark times when God stood by us and made a 'way of escape' is a source of nourishment to continue in faith. In fact, Hebrews 10:32–39 encourages us to think back to previous times of suffering when we find ourselves entering difficult times:

> Remember those earlier days after you had received the light, when you stood your ground in a great contest in the face of suffering. Sometimes you were publicly exposed to insult and persecution; at other times you stood side by side with those who were so treated. You sympathised with those in prison and joyfully accepted the confiscation of your property, because you knew that you yourselves had better and lasting possessions.
>
> So do not throw away your confidence; it will be richly rewarded. You need to persevere so that when you have done the will of God, you will receive what he has promised. For in just a very little while, 'He who is coming will come and will not delay. But my righteous one will live by faith. And if he shrinks back, I will not be pleased with him.' But we are not of those who shrink back and are destroyed, but of those who believe and are saved.

Coming Up Higher

Read

1 Corinthians 4:3–5; Psalm 139:23,24; Romans 8:17;
2 Corinthians 1:5; chapter 2

Reflect

Paul says in 1 Corinthians 4:3–5 that we shouldn't be
concerned about what other people think about us, because
the One who examines us is the Lord. Are you concerned
about what others think about you?

Sometimes we need to ask God to search our hearts (Psalm
139:23,24). Ask God to show you if there is any sin in your
life. What did He show you?

God's correction is something all of us need. In which of the
following ways do you respond to God's corrections?
• Drop out
• Hang in there but never grow up
• Own up to your less-than-Christlike character
Why do people struggle to admit their mistakes (sins) instead
of agreeing with God that nobody is perfect?

What do the following verses teach about the necessity of
suffering: Romans 8:17; 2 Corinthians 1:5; 2 Timothy 2:9–13?

Respond

Almighty and all powerful and holy God, I rejoice in Your
unfailing love and perfect plan. I praise You for the hope and
comfort I find in You and in the fact that You know pain. I
thank You, too, for the fact that You use and redeem the
suffering of my life and for the ways You've taken care of me
in the past. When trials, pain and suffering come again, help
me cast my cares upon You and once again know Your grace.
And Lord, I never want to doubt in darkness what I have
learned about You and Your goodness. I pray in the name of
Your holy Son, amen.

Notes

Introduction: The Treasure

1. Charles Swindoll, *The Living Insights Study Bible* (Grand Rapids, MI: Zondervan, 1996), p 1203.

Chapter 1: Life-Changing Stuff

1. Max Lucado, *The Inspirational Study Bible, God's Love* (Dallas: Word, 1995).
2. Wayne Rice, 'Medical Terms You Need to Know', *More Hot Illustrations for Youth Talks* (Grand Rapids, MI: Zondervan, 1995), p 116.
3. Wayne Rice, 'The Smartest Teenager in the World', *Hot Illustrations for Youth Talks* (El Cajon, CA: Youth Specialties, 1994), p 182.
4. Rice, 'Medical Terms', p 114.
5. Jim Burns and Greg McKinnon, 'Is Anybody Else Up There?' *Illustrations, Stories and Quotes You Can Hang Your Message On* (Ventura, CA: Gospel Light, 1997), p 113.

Chapter 2: The Power of Truth

1. Henry T. Blackaby, *The Power of the Call* (Nashville: Broadman and Holman, 1997), p 127.
2. Jim Burns and Greg McKinnon, 'She Knows Her Own', *Illustrations, Stories and Quotes You Can Hang Your Message On* (Ventura, CA: Gospel Light, 1997), p 33.
3. To help you work through your problems and concerns, Freedom in Christ Ministries has developed the 'Steps to Freedom'. These steps can be found in our book *Bondage Breakers, Youth Edition*, or you can write to us for them: Freedom in Christ Ministries, 491 E Lambert Road, La Habra, CA 90631 or check out our web sites: www.freedominchrist.com; www.ficyouth.com.
4. Paul Meier, 'Spiritual and Mental Health in the Balance' in *Renewing Your Mind in a Secular World*, John D. Woodbridge, ed. (Chicago: Moody Press, 1985), pp 26–28.

Chapter 3: The Power of Our Actions

1. Joseph Stowell, *Perilous Pursuits* (Chicago: Moody Press, 1994), p 99.
2. Peter T. O'Brien, *Colossians, Philemon*, The Word Biblical Commentary, vol. 44 (Waco, TX: Word, 1982), p 23.
3. Taken from David G. Myers, *The Human Puzzle* (San Francisco: Harper and Row, 1978), p 97.
4. Jim Burns and Greg McKinnon, 'The Praying Hands', *Illustrations, Stories and Quotes You Can Hang Your Message On* (Ventura, CA: Gospel Light, 1997), p 163.
5. Cited by Bruce Larson, *A Call to Holy Living*.

Chapter 4: What About God's Rules?

1. Charles Swindoll, *Growing Deep in the Christian Life* (Portland, OR: Multnomah Press, 1993), p 418.
2. Wayne Rice, 'The New Gorilla', *More Hot Illustrations for Youth Talks* (Grand Rapids, MI: Zondervan, 1995), p 127.
3. Ibid., 'The Mud Flats', p 121.
4. A. van Selms, *The New Bible Dictionary*, J. D. Douglas, ed. (Grand Rapids, MI: Eerdmans, 1962), s.v. 'law'.
5. W. J. Harrelson, 'Law in the OT', *The Interpreter's Dictionary of the Bible*, George A. Buttrick, ed. (Nashville: Abingdon, 1976), 3:77.
6. While the law in Matthew 5:17 is a reference to the Old Testament law, Christ being a fulfilment of the Old Testament law also encompasses *all* of God's law, including that written *in the hearts of all people* (see Romans 2:15). For a brief discussion on the meaning of Christ as the 'fulfilment' and 'end' of the law, see Douglas J. Moo, 'The Law of Moses of the Law of Christ', in *Continuity and Discontinuity*, John S. Feinberg, ed. (Westchester, IL: Crossway Books, 1988), pp 203–18.
7. Horatius Bonar, *God's Way of Holiness* (Phillipsburg, NJ: Presbyterian and Reformed Publishing, 1979), p 120.
8. Ibid., pp 41–42.

Chapter 5: Abiding in Christ

1. Philip Yancey, *The Jesus I Never Knew* (Grand Rapids, MI: Zondervan, 1995).
2. Wayne Rice, 'How Embarrassing', *More Hot Illustrations for Youth Talks* (Grand Rapids, MI: Zondervan, 1995), p 88.

3. Ibid, 'Great Answers but No Help', p 78.
4. Ibid, 'The Lantern', p 104.
5. We have chosen to use the NASB throughout this discussion of abiding in Christ because it uses the word *abide* rather than *remain* as in the NIV. *Abide* is more accurate at this point and adds intimacy and a dynamic that is not clear in 'remain'.
6. Raymond E. Brown, *The Gospel According to John* (i–xii), The Anchor Bible (Garden City, NY: Doubleday, 1966), vol. 29, pp 510–11. Karlfried Munzer, *The New International Dictionary of New Testament Theology*, Colin Brown, ed. (Grand Rapids, MI: Zondervan, 1971), vol. 3, s.v. 'remain'.
7. Rice, 'Chippie's Bad Day', *More Hot Illustrations*, p 51.

Chapter 6: Filled with the Spirit

1. Jack Hayford, gen. ed., *Hayford's Bible Handbook* (Nashville: Thomas Nelson, 1995), p 377.
2. Neil T. Anderson, *Walking in the Light* (Nashville: Thomas Nelson, 1992), adapted from pp 173–74.
3. F. J. Helfmeyer, *Theological Dictionary of the Old Testament*, G. Johannes Botterweck and Helmer Ringgren, eds. (Grand Rapids, MI: Eerdmans, 1978), vol. 3, p 390.
4. E. Edmond Hiebert, *The Thessalonian Epistles* (Chicago: Moody Press, 1971), p 244. For more on the general applicability of the command, see also Leon Morris, *The First and Second Epistles to the Thessalonians*, rev. ed. (Grand Rapids, Eerdmans, 1968), p 291.
5. Wayne Rice, 'A Vision of Jesus', *More Hot Illustrations for Youth Talks* (Grand Rapids, MI: Zondervan, 1995), p 27.
6. Gerhard Delling, *Theological Dictionary of the New Testament*, Gerhard Friedrich, ed. (Grand Rapids, MI: Eerdmans, 1968), p 291.
7. Rice, 'The President and the Little Boy', *More Hot Illustrations*, p 140.
8. Ibid., 'Save the Starfish', p 151.
9. A. W. Tozer, *Gems from Tozer* (Camp Hill, PA: Christian Publications, 1969), pp 68–69.

Chapter 7: Growing in Holiness

1. Wayne Rice, 'Smart Hopis', *More Hot Illustrations for Youth Talks* (Grand Rapids, MI: Zondervan, 1995), p 158.

2. Wayne Rice, *Hot Illustrations for Youth Talks* (El Cajon, CA: Youth Specialties, 1994), p 40.
3. Ibid., 'The Hermit's Gift', p 112.
4. Howard Hendricks, 'I don't believe a word of it', *More Stories for the Heart*, Alice Gray, comp. (Sisters, OR: Multnomah, 1997), p 46.

Chapter 8: The Struggle

1. John Stott, *The Message of Galatians* (London: InterVarsity Press, 1968), p 151.
2. Markus Barth, 'Ephesians 4 – 6', *The Anchor Bible* (Garden City, NY: Doubleday, 1974), p 763; see also Ephesians 6:10–16.
3. Wayne Rice, 'A Diet for Losers', *More Hot Illustrations for Youth Talks* (Grand Rapids, MI: Zondervan, 1995), p 21.
4. Ibid., 'The Reasonable Hunter', p 146.
5. Wayne Rice, 'The Blood of an Overcomer', *Hot Illustrations for Youth Talks* (El Cajon, CA: Youth Specialties, 1994), p 42.
6. J. Behm, *Theological Dictionary of the New Testament*, Colin Brown, ed. (Grand Rapids, MI: Eerdmans, 1982), vol. 4, p 161.

Chapter 9: Warfare!

1. Peter Davids, *The Epistle of James* (Grand Rapids, MI: Eerdmans, 1982), pp 161–66.
2. To help you work through your problems and concerns, Freedom in Christ Ministries has developed the 'Steps to Freedom'. These steps can be found in our book *Bondage Breakers, Youth Edition*, or you can write to us for them: Freedom in Christ Ministries, 491 E Lambert Road, La Habra, CA 90631 or check out our web sites: www.freedominchrist.com; www.ficyouth.com.
3. Norval Geldenhuys, *Commentary on the Gospel of Luke* (Grand Rapids, MI: Eerdmans, 1951), p 566.
4. Hiebert says, 'The present participle ['the tempter' in 1 Thessalonians 3:5] pictures him as persistently engaged in the effort to destroy the faith of the Thessalonians through temptation. He never gives up his sinister efforts.' See D. Edmond Hiebert, *The Thessalonian Epistles* (Chicago: Moody Press, 1971), p 142.
5. Most interpreters see *evil* as personal, that is, *evil one*. In Matthew it would be naturally associated with Satan, who is called the 'tempter'.

6. Andrew T. Lincoln, 'Ephesians', *World Biblical Commentary* (Dallas: Word Books, 1990), vol. 42, p 433.
7. Wayne Rice, 'Wolf Hunters', *Hot Illustrations for Youth Talks* (El Cajon, CA: Youth Specialties, 1994), p 87.
8. The term *spirit* in Ephesians 2:2 is taken to refer directly to Satan (see Markus Barth, 'Ephesians 1 – 3', *Anchor Bible* [Garden City, NY: Doubleday, 1974], pp 22–29). It may also refer to the evil spiritual power over which Satan rules (see Lincoln, 'Ephesians', pp 96–97) or as 'a term describing the empire of spirits over whom Satan presides' (see John Eadie, *Commentary on the Epistle to the Ephesians* [Grand Rapids, MI: Zondervan, 1883], p 123). In any case, it refers to the evil-spirit power at work in those who belong to the world.
9. J. Armitage Robinson, *St Paul's Epistle to the Ephesians* (London: James Clarke, n.d.), p 155.
10. Note also 1 Corinthians 2:12, where the spirit of the world is contrasted to the Spirit from God.
11. Other passages that connect the flesh and demonic influence are seen throughout Scripture. Evil thoughts come from our own heart (Matthew 15:19). Yet they also stem from Satan, as we have seen in the cases of David and Ananias. Satan tempts the believer to lack of self-control in the area of sexuality, which, in some passages, refers to the desires of the flesh (for example, 1 Corinthians 7:3–5). As Grosheide explains, '… The incontinence exists always and everywhere and seeks expression. Satan uses it by urging people to give it an illicit expression. And then sin is near' (F. W. Grosheide, *Commentary on the First Epistle to the Corinthians* [Grand Rapids, MI: Eerdmans, 1953], p 158). David Powlison notes, 'Satan's congruence with the fallen human heart operates in every passage that deals with moral evil. See Ephesians, 1 Peter, 1 Timothy 3:6, 1 Corinthians 10:6–11 and 1 John 3:1–10 and 5:16–21' (David Powlison, *Power Encounters* [Grand Rapids, MI: Baker Book House, 1994], p 159, n. 17).
12. George W. Knight III, 'The Pastoral Epistles', *New International Greek Testament Commentary* (Grand Rapids, MI: Eerdmans, 1992), p 166.
13. For more information about repentance and key steps you can follow, see Neil and Dave's book *Stomping Out the Darkness*. The nature of spiritual conflicts and the biblical principle of repentance, what we call the 'Steps to Freedom', are taught in Neil and Dave's book *Bondage Breakers, Youth Edition*.

14. J. Ramsey Michaels, '1 Peter', *Word Biblical Commentary* (Waco, TX: Word Books, 1988), vol. 49, p 300.
15. Edward G. Selwyn, *The First Epistle of St Peter* (London: MacMillan, 1961), p 238.

Chapter 10: When the Going Gets Tough

1. C. S. Lewis, *The Problem of Pain* (New York: MacMillan, 1962), p 93.
2. Wayne Rice, 'When Nothing Goes Right', *More Hot Illustrations for Youth Talks* (Grand Rapids, MI: Zondervan, 1995), p 173.
3. Rice, 'Blackouts', *More Hot Illustrations*, p 44.
4. Wayne Rice, 'The Emperor Moth', *Hot Illustrations for Youth Talks* (El Cajon, CA: Youth Specialties, 1994), p 85.